Runoff Elections
in the United States

The Thornton H. Brooks Series

in American Law and Society

The University of North Carolina Press

Chapel Hill and London

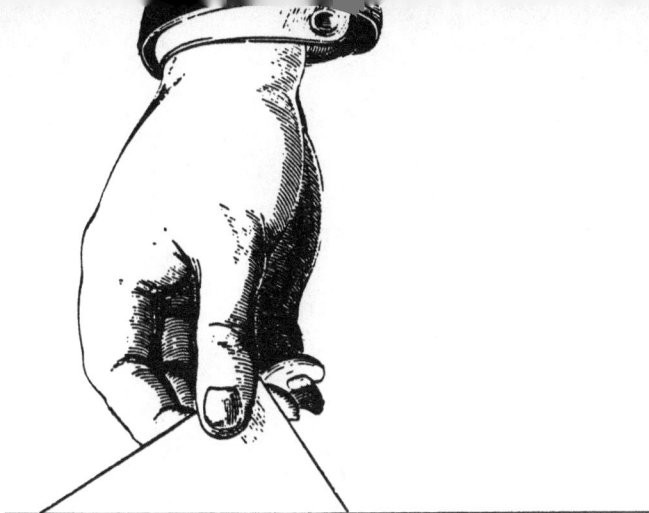

Runoff Elections in the United States

Charles S. Bullock III

and Loch K. Johnson

Library of Congress Cataloging-in-Publication Data
Bullock, Charles S., 1942–
    Runoff elections in the United States / Charles S. Bullock, Loch K.
Johnson.
        p.   cm.—(The Thornton H. Brooks series in American law and
society)
    Includes bibliographical references (p.   ) and index.
    ISBN 9780807865156 (pbk. : alk. paper)
    1. Elections—United States.   2. Voting—United States.
    3. Representative government and representation—United States.
    4. Afro-Americans—Politics and government.   I. Johnson, Loch K.,
    1942–   . II. Title. III. Series.
    JK1976.B77   1992
    324.6'0973—dc20   92-53626
                                                               CIP

Some of the data in chapter 1 have been published previously in a
substantially different form in Charles S. Bullock III and Loch K.
Johnson, "The Incidence of Runoff Primaries," in Laurence W. Moreland
et al., *Blacks in Southern Politics.* © 1987 by Greenwood Press,
Praeger Publishers. Reprinted by permission of Greenwood Publishing
Group, Inc. Chapter 2 has been published previously in a substantially
different form in the following journals and is reprinted with permission
of the University of Texas Press: Charles S. Bullock III and Loch K.
Johnson, "Runoff Elections in Georgia," *Journal of Politics* 47, no. 3
(August 1985): 937–46; Charles S. Bullock III and Loch K. Johnson,
"Sex and the Second Primary," *Social Science Quarterly* 66, no. 4
(December 1985): 933–44.

To the memories of

Cortez A. M. Ewing

and V. O. Key, Jr.,

with lasting admiration

Contents

Tables

Preface

Nothing is more important to the vitality, indeed the survival, of a democracy—that rare and fragile form of government in which the views of the people count—than free and open elections. In addition, true democracies feature an unfettered media, due process, fair trials, protected speech and privacy, and, in the more robust, mature variants, equal opportunities for economic and social advancement, with no citizen relegated to deprivation. Yet, in the absence of competitive elections—the guardian angel of liberty—these additional benefits of democracy are unlikely to survive.

Given the importance of elections to democratic government, political scientists have devoted a good deal of attention to this subject. The professional literature abounds with detailed studies of voting behavior, political parties, campaign strategies, nominating conventions, the influence of media on elections, the contemporary effects of the Electoral College, and the like. The most impressive contribution of American scholars to the discipline of political science may well be, in fact, the rich understanding of elections that has emerged from their research in the second half of this century.

Although the scholarly literature is impressive, the search for knowledge about electoral behavior in democracies, both here and abroad, has by no means been completed. Much of the underbrush has been cleared away, but the jungle remains dark and deep. The findings offered in this volume seek to contribute to this search by addressing a little-studied, yet important, method of leadership selection: the runoff primary.

The runoff has been tried in seventeen states and is presently used in ten southern states and two states outside the South (for a listing, see Table 1.1

in chapter 1). A large number of municipalities across the country have also adopted the runoff procedure (some for nominations, others for elections), and it was even embraced in the former Soviet Union for local elections under the new wave of democracy that began to sweep the U.S.S.R. in 1989–90. Under the runoff rule, a candidate for public office usually must win nomination by majority vote—a bow to the time-honored deference to the will of the majority in democratic regimes. If a candidate fails to attract a majority of the votes in a first election, he or she is required to stand against the second-place finisher in another round of balloting. In this second (or "runoff") contest, the winning candidate is assured a majority victory.

Using advanced mathematical models, specialists on the intricacies of voting behavior have demonstrated that the majoritarian objectives of the runoff procedure can never be fully realized in practice. In some voting patterns, a *Condorcet Paradox* can arise (named after the French mathematician who discovered this phenomenon, Marquis de Condorcet, 1743–94). In these instances, it is possible for a candidate to be eliminated in a runoff primary system even though in head-to-head, one-on-one competition he or she would be able to defeat all comers.[1]

Even though the runoff primary can result in an unfair outcome on some occasions, this electoral method is less likely to produce the Condorcet Paradox than is a plurality system. As Samuel Merrill has observed, the runoff's major virtue over a plurality system is the likelihood that a second primary will lead to "the selection of the candidate with the broadest appeal."[2] Nevertheless, Merrill prefers the technique of *approval voting* over the runoff. With this procedure, each voter is allowed to vote for as many candidates as he or she wishes but may cast only one ballot per candidate. The candidate who garners the most votes is the winner.[3]

The Condorcet Paradox and the merits of approval voting both warrant the attention of students interested in electoral behavior; but, we must emphasize at the beginning, they are not our subjects. Rather, the purpose of this volume is to examine a range of empirical findings and political controversies related to the runoff method alone.

In chapter 1, we set the stage for an empirical analysis of the runoff by describing in greater detail its raison d'être, briefly outlining its evolution and explaining its current importance in the United States as a method for leadership selection. Why is it that a second electoral contest, with all the added costs and administrative rigmarole involved, has been adopted by so many electoral constituencies? Why haven't these party officials simply relied on a single election, with the nominee being that candidate who garners a plurality of the total number of votes cast—the first across the line wins, without an exhausting (both physically and fiscally) second race among the top two contenders? A single nominating election is, after all, the method used in most contests for public office in the United States.

As part of our introduction to the runoff, we include in this opening chapter fresh data on the frequency (or incidence) of runoffs. Our purpose here is to clarify those conditions under which a second primary is likely to occur. The orienting questions here are, How often do runoffs take place, and what configuration of electoral variables present in a first primary is most likely to necessitate a second primary in order to produce a clear-cut winner preferred by a majority of the voters? Put another way, what electoral circumstances reduce the likelihood of a majority-vote outcome in the first primary? Among the considerations in our analysis are whether an incumbent is one of the candidates and whether the office seekers are black or white, male or female.

In chapter 2, we turn to several propositions—myths, in our view—that have become mainstays in the conventional wisdom about runoff primaries. According to the first, which we call the "leader-loses" myth, the winner of the initial primary is likely to lose in the runoff. The underlying assumption is that those candidates eliminated in the opening round will join forces to defeat the front-runner once they have been plied with assurances from the second-place candidate of patronage, policy adoptions, and, most important, campaign debt absorption (a "reimbursement of expenses" or, as V. O. Key put it in a graceful euphemism, a "consideration"). The second-place finishers also may benefit from a certain amount of voter sympathy for their underdog status.

A second proposition—the "incumbent-loses" myth—argues that incumbents, if so weak among their constituents as to be forced into a runoff, are likely to fail in their bid for reelection. We test the validity of this assertion at various levels of office.

The next two myths that have grown up around the dual-primary system deal with sex and race. Why has the dual-primary system provoked such controversy in recent years, igniting a public debate fueled by charges of gender and racial discrimination? How valid are the allegations leveled by critics that the runoff carries with it an inherently antifemale and antiblack bias? In our search for answers to these questions, we first analyze the widely assumed pernicious effects of the runoff on the electoral prospects of women— the "female-loses" myth. Feminist leader Eleanor Smeal, among others, has roundly criticized the runoff as a detriment to women winning public office. In chapter 2, we study the extent to which female candidates may have, in fact, been blocked from office by defeat in a second primary.

In chapters 3 and 4, we explore the relationship between the race of would-be nominees and their fate in the second primary. The conventional wisdom regards the runoff as an imposing barrier to black candidates in black-white competitions. Supposedly, racially motivated white voters will unite to defeat a black candidate in the second primary—the "minority-loses" myth.

We start our probe into the racial aspect of the dual-primary system with a qualitative analysis of recent court decisions that have addressed the runoff primary, one handed down in the city of New York and another in the state of Arkansas. The arguments in these key cases distill much of the debate that has arisen over the implications of a candidate's skin color for his or her chances under double-primary rule. Although most of this book relies on a macroanalysis of aggregate data from across the South, chapter 3 offers a microlevel look at concrete examples of the runoff in action. The New York City and Arkansas experiences provide a sense of the variety and texture of specific dual-primary contests—at a distance from one another of 1,500 miles and in dramatically different political and cultural settings.

In chapter 4, we return to the aggregate analysis, bringing to bear new data on the relationship between race and the runoff. Rev. Jesse Jackson, the most prominent black leader in the United States and twice an aspirant for the presidency (1984 and 1988), has frequently criticized the dual-primary system for its alleged discriminatory effects. Drawing on our aggregate data, this chapter assesses Jackson's critique.

In chapter 5, we explore the recent runoff experiences in North Carolina, which has experimented with changing the voting thresholds necessary to trigger a second primary. In chapter 6, we provide data on the degree of voter turnout in runoff primaries, as well as on the impact that runoffs have on general elections. Lastly, in chapter 7 we appraise the future of the runoff in U.S. elections.

Acknowledgments

We would like to thank a number of individuals for their assistance in this project. Our students Randy Austin, Don Dye, Keith Gaddie, John Kuzinski, Anthony Moussios, David Price, Bobby Reid, Margaret Schuelke, and A. Brock Smith helped with the data collection. The Honorable Glen Browder, now an Alabama congressman, secured his state's election data for us in his earlier capacity as secretary of state. Robert Montjoy provided some of the Alabama data on race, and Del Dunn helped us gain access to several years of the Mississippi data. Diana Blair, Jason Kirksen, Dick Murray, Joe Stewart, and Tom Vocino were able to identify additional black candidates for us. Earl Black, Merle Black, Malcolm E. Jewell, Lee Johnston, Lloyd Jones, William R. Keech, Susan A. MacManus, and Harold W. Stanley offered expert consultation along the way. Bridget Pilcher did most of the typing.

Paul Betz and Sandra Eisdorfer, our editors at the University of North Carolina Press, provided excellent editorial guidance. The editors of the *Journal of Politics, Social Science Quarterly*, and *Blacks in Southern Politics* (New York: Praeger, 1987) permitted us to draw upon our previously published work on this topic. The curators of the Western History Collection at the University of Oklahoma kindly allowed us to examine and integrate into this study Cortez A. M. Ewing's original handwritten data from his classic runoff research of 1953. And the Bullock and Johnson clans once again showed great patience with their two scribblers.

Runoff Elections

in the United States

Then one day Willie woke up and found himself running for Governor. Or rather, he was running in the Democratic primary, which in our state is the same as running for Governor.—Robert Penn Warren, *All the King's Men*

1 Introduction

The runoff primary has been variously dubbed the "second primary," the "second ballot," the "double primary," the "run-over primary," or the "dual-primary system." A primary is an electoral contest held to choose a party's nominee for public office. The nominees selected in this manner by the various parties (in the United States, usually the Democratic and Republican parties) then stand before the public in a final vote, which determines the officeholder. At the turn of the century, reformer-leaders of the Progressive movement advocated the primary as a means for opening up the process of leadership selection to rank-and-file voters. Before the advent of the primary, party bosses had enjoyed the luxury of handpicking their favorite nominees—often mere toadies—through secret negotiations in the now-legendary smoke-filled (and bourbon-scented) back rooms of party headquarters.

Under the runoff variation of the primary, if no candidate for nomination receives a majority of the votes cast, he or she is then required to face the second-place finisher in another election held a few weeks later (the runoff). In this narrowed two-person contest, the eventual nominee is guaranteed the opportunity to boast of majority support within his or her party, rather than having to confront the opposition party in the general election with a weaker plurality vote—indeed, perhaps only a sliver of victory in the balloting for nomination.

The Runoff in Historical Perspective

In plurality elections, the candidate who receives more votes than anyone else is declared the victor—the first past the post wins all. In contrast, the democratic principle underlying the runoff is majoritarian: a legitimate nominee should represent a majority of the party's membership, not, say, only one-fourth, with 75 percent of the party's voting strength discounted.[1] The voters in Arkansas became distressed in 1937, for instance, by the results of their plurality election for governor. Carl E. Bailey won the Democratic nomination (and, in this one-party state, thereby assured himself election) with a vote of less than 32 percent of the total in a five-man race.[2] Soon after this controversial election, the voters of Arkansas adopted the runoff provision on a permanent basis (having experimented with it off and on since 1933).

A latecomer to the runoff system, Arkansas was among the last states to adopt this approach (see Table 1.1). As two-party competition disappeared throughout the South at the turn of the century, the runoff movement spread. With all the serious candidates competing in the Democratic party primary, a relatively small fraction of the vote might constitute a winning plurality. Earl Black has determined that at the gubernatorial level, most southern states have been multifactional.[3] In a multicandidate primary, the leader of a regional or extreme ideological bloc might poll the most votes, even though most of the electorate preferred any of several alternatives to the front-runner. Southerners turned to the runoff as a means for ensuring that the Democratic nominee was the preference of a majority of the voters—though, for some, the rule may have had the purpose of protecting segregationist policies as well.[4]

Seventeen states, mostly in or bordering on the South, have experimented with the runoff method at one time or another, beginning with Mississippi in 1902 up to Arizona in 1988 (Kentucky's flirtation lasted only from 1935 to 1936). Some states initially embraced a majority-rule requirement through party rules (Georgia and South Carolina, for example). Ten southern states have adopted the runoff as a long-term feature of their statewide electoral landscapes. Along with Mississippi, these states include Alabama, Arkansas, Florida, Georgia, Louisiana, North Carolina, Oklahoma, South Carolina, Tennessee, and Texas. (If two contenders tie in its second primary, South Carolina even has a third-primary provision.) Three states outside the South also established a runoff procedure: Maryland, briefly, South Dakota and Utah more enthusiastically, and—in an odd twist of the normal runoff procedure—Arizona most recently in gubernatorial general elections (see Table 1.1).[5] Fur-

Table 1.1 State Adoption of the Runoff

State	Year of Formal Adoption	Modified	Abandoned
Mississippi	1902		
Texas	1903		
North Carolina	1915	1989	
South Carolina	1915		
Georgia	1917	1964	
Louisiana	1922	1975	
Florida	1929		
Maryland	1929*		1939
Oklahoma	1929		
South Dakota	1929*	1973	
Alabama	1931		
Arkansas	1933, 1939		1935–38
Kentucky	1935*		1936
Tennessee	1937*		
Utah	1937*		1947
Virginia	1952*		1969
Arizona	1988**		

Sources: Joe Park, "The Elusive Majority," *National Municipal Review*, October 1940, p. 675; Louise Overacker, "Direct Primary Legislation, 1936–1939," *American Political Science Review* (June 1940): 503–6; Henry M. Alexander, "The Double Primary," *Arkansas Historical Quarterly* 3 (Autumn 1944): 219–22; V. O. Key, Jr., *Southern Politics in State and Nation* (New York: Knopf, 1949), p. 417, n. 18; Cortez A. M. Ewing, *Primary Elections in the South: A Study in Uniparty Politics* (Norman: University of Oklahoma, 1953), pp. 8–9; Rick Huffe, executive director, South Dakota Democratic party, telephone interview with authors, March 8, 1990; Jan Schoonmaker, legislative assistant, office of Representative Lindy Boggs (D-La.), telephone interview with authors, March 13, 1990; Karen Osborn, Arizona assistant secretary of state, telephone interview with authors, September 11, 1990; John T. Willis, *Presidential Elections in Maryland* (Mt. Airy, Md.: Lemond, 1984), p. 95.
*Excluded from this study because of their abandonment of the dual-primary system (Kentucky, Maryland, Utah, and Virginia), atypical runoff rules (Tennessee), or lack of use (Arizona and South Dakota).
**Required in general elections for selected statewide offices; not used in primaries.

ther, in hundreds of cities across the land the double primary has become a permanent fixture in the nominating process (for one example, New York City, see chapter 5).

In Tennessee, a runoff is employed only in the unlikely case of a tie; therefore, it is excluded from this analysis, along with the four states that have abandoned the runoff altogether: Kentucky, Maryland, Utah, and Virginia. (In 1990 the Kentucky senate adopted a runoff rule in the case of contests for governor and lieutenant governor, but the measure failed in the house.) South Dakota must be omitted too, as officials in this state have yet to use this method.

In Arizona, interest in the runoff sprang from the impeachment in 1988 of Governor Evan Mecham (for obstructing an investigation of his staff). In the future, reformers hoped to avoid the election of candidates with narrowly based support by turning to a runoff procedure. The state legislature chose, however, to establish a runoff only *after* no candidate received a majority in the general election (say, in a three-person race). This rule—hastily written and containing many ambiguous features, such as exactly how long after a "deadlocked" general election the runoff would be held—applies to all statewide elections. The specifics were worked out in 1990, when an Independent candidate kept the Democratic and Republican gubernatorial nominees below 50 percent of the vote.

Louisiana employs a unique open-primary system, followed by a nonpartisan second primary that can serve as the general election. Created by Act 1 of the state legislature in 1975, this system provides that all candidates for a given office—regardless of party—will be placed on the same ballot for the primary contests. If one candidate receives a simple majority in the first primary, he or she is declared the winner of the office; hence, there is no general election in the traditional sense. Often, however, no candidate receives a simple majority in this initial competition (especially for gubernatorial and federal legislative offices). In these instances, the top two vote getters— regardless of party affiliation—are placed in a scheduled second primary. This race is called the "runoff election," even though it is essentially Louisiana's equivalent of the general election.

The Louisiana primary system is the only one in the United States that allows for the possibility that two candidates from the same party might face each other in the "general election," as could have occurred in the 1987 gubernatorial race. Incumbent governor Edwin W. Edwards and U.S. Representative Charles ("Buddy") Roemer, both Democrats, garnered the most votes in the opening primary among a field of five other Democrats and U.S. Representative Robert L. Livingston, a Republican. Consequently, Edwards and Roemer faced the prospect of a general election pitting Democrat against Democrat. Edwards decided to drop out of the race, making Roemer the winner by default.

In an attempt to maximize its opportunities for success under this system, the Louisiana State Republican Party adopted an unwritten law to support only one GOP candidate in most major elections. Republican would-be office-holders are free to run in these races, of course, but party discipline is normally strong enough to dissuade such "renegade" behavior. Often in the more important contests, the Democratic vote is fragmented among several candidates, while the Republican vote remains relatively solid.

In 1990 two Republicans challenged the incumbent Democratic senator, Bennett Johnston. The choice of mainstreamer Ben Baggett by the GOP failed to dissuade former Ku Klux Klan leader David Duke, who in 1989 had won a special election to the Louisiana legislature as a Republican, from entering the race. On the eve of the election, when it appeared that a Johnston-Duke runoff was likely, Baggett withdrew. Unlike the more common scenario in which the GOP rallies behind one candidate to enhance the party's chances, Baggett withdrew to ensure Bennett's first-round victory, as Duke's uninvited presence in the party had embarrassed many GOP regulars in Louisiana and elsewhere.

Much of Louisiana, like many portions of the rest of the South, remains staunchly Democratic. Therefore, in the typical Louisiana second election, two Democrats square off with the winner taking office, just as occurred during the heyday of one-partyism. Occasionally, as in the special election won by David Duke in the suburbs of New Orleans, the runoff is between a pair of Republicans. Only for the more visible offices, such as governor, is it common for the second election to resemble a general election in which candidates of opposing parties compete. Unless the Democratic candidate is "caught in bed with a dead girl or a live boy" (to borrow one of Governor

Edwards's more famous comments), most Democratic voters then support the only remaining Democrat in the race, leaving the GOP contender to face relatively great odds against victory.

The Appeal of Majority Voting

Proponents of the second-primary system emphasize how the tallying of a majority vote, made possible even in a crowded field by adoption of the runoff procedure, adds legitimacy to a nomination. A second primary encourages a candidate to broaden his or her appeal between the initial primary and the runoff by eschewing narrow stands on the campaign issues. Once the winner assumes office, this can lead to even greater responsiveness across a wider range of constituent demands. Moreover, the impression of a strong, broadly supported candidate emerging from the pack with majority support enhances the image of the nominee as a popular figure—always helpful to a party as it appeals for wider voter support in the general election. The runoff is lauded, in a word, for the majority support it "manufactures."[6]

Runoff proponents also stress that plurality voting without a runoff encourages the politics of extreme factionalism—rule by small cliques or rabble-rousers rather than by individuals who are broadly acceptable to the electorate.[7] The rise of the Ku Klux Klan in the South spurred interest in the runoff provision in at least one state as a way to consolidate anti-Klan voters behind a more moderate candidate in a second primary.[8] If nominations were made simply by plurality vote, a candidate relying on the solid support of the Klan (or some other extremist group) could conceivably snatch victory from the hands of a crowded field of contenders—including some candidates more widely acceptable to the electorate—with only a small percentage of the total vote. As a prominent Arkansas politician recalled at mid-century: "There is a connection between the Klan practice of uniting behind one of its own members and the agitation (in 1924) for a run-off [in Arkansas] so that the anti-Klan vote would not be divided."[9]

The Emergence of a One-Party South

The major risk associated with a single-primary system based on plurality voting—the emergence of successful splinter (sometimes extremist) candidates—has loomed as a particularly troubling prospect throughout the South. Since the turn of the century, the Democratic party has dominated this region—until recently. (Even now the party monopolizes most federal and state offices and has complete control in most rural areas, despite Republican successes in presidential elections and impressive inroads at the state level and in selected localities). Democratic dominance evolved in the post–Reconstruction era from the party's stance on white supremacy, which was popular among Negrophobes—though for a time between the end of the Civil War in 1865 and 1890 both the Democratic and Republican parties courted the black voter. In large part, the Democratic party turned against blacks, paradoxically, as a result of the Populist movement in the South, which—at first— championed the cause of the black man and woman. Agrarian reformer Tom Watson, of Georgia, America's most prominent Populist, took the lead in trying to build a political coalition of poor whites and blacks against the wealthy plantation owners and emerging southern industrialists, that is, against the conservative wing of the Democratic party.

Alarmed by this prospect ("potential black supremacy was the nightmare of the white Piedmont and hill citizenry," noted Cortez A. M. Ewing),[10] the conservatives sought to drive a wedge between the black and white components of Watson's coalition through race-baiting. Further, conservative plantation owners ordered black workers under their control to vote against the Populist candidates and for proponents of white supremacy. As C. Vann Woodward writes, "Some [of these black workers] were merely counted for the ticket, however they voted or whether they voted or not. Time after time the Populists would discover that after they had carried the white counties, fraudulent returns from the black belt counties padded with ballots the Negro did or did not cast were used to overwhelm them."[11] The Populists found their attempts to rally poor blacks further frustrated by Jim Crow voting laws, like the poll tax Georgia enacted in 1877, which made access to the polls for the underclass (including almost all blacks) virtually impossible.

Watson and other leading Populists soon gave up their original goal of bonding poor whites and blacks into a powerful coalition. Instead, they turned to what seemed a more realistic objective: the rallying of poor whites to their reformist crusade against the propertied class. This meant a sharp about-face in their championship of poor blacks; quite the opposite, Watson and others adopted a strategy of further whipping up the antiblack sentiment already provoked by the wealthy Bourbon faction. "Both the conservatives and the Populists shifted to the cause of white supremacy," concludes Everett Carll Ladd, Jr.; "instead of poor whites against more prosperous whites, it became whites against blacks."[12] The Republican party, hated for its Reconstruction policies and problack initiatives, was poorly situated to compete against the Democrats for the white vote. The GOP sunk quickly over the horizon as a serious alternative to the Democratic party in the South.

In the twentieth century, the Democratic party remained dominant throughout the South. It did so even as national Democrats began earnestly and successfully to woo black voters during Franklin Roosevelt's New Deal era and after—through the weight of inertia, tradition, and the recruitment of popular local candidates for office. In this ongoing one-party or uniparty situation, the nomination phase continued to be all-important, with the general election usually more of a coronation of the successful Democratic nominee than a genuine electoral contest between parties. (Again, this is changing, as Republicans capture an increasing number of offices in the contemporary South.)[13]

In sum, until the last decade or so, whoever won the Democratic primary in the South won office; thus, the intraparty struggle became the critical event. With a single-primary system, a small bloc of party activists—the Klan, for instance—could control the outcome. In seeking to avoid this rule-by-minority-faction, southern party reformers found the runoff proposal attractive.

Researching the Runoff

The runoff remains a largely unstudied phenomenon, despite its use by a fifth of the states as well as hundreds of cities and despite the criticism by Rev. Jesse L. Jackson and others that has been reported extensively in the media.[14] The only notable early effort to come to grips with the runoff in any systematic way was reflected in a single book chapter published in 1953 by Cortez A. M. Ewing, a political scientist at the University of Oklahoma. Ewing examined second primaries from 1920 through 1948 (excluding Georgia).[15] We hope to fill this research gap by drawing upon a newly collected data set—one that includes runoff elections from the ten southern states where this procedure has been in steady use from 1970 through 1986 (see Table 1.1)—as well as by reexamining data gathered by others.

Our principal data cover runoffs held from 1970 to 1986 to fill statewide, congressional, and state-level legislative and executive offices—1,222 runoffs. Judicial positions were excluded, as were special elections to fill interim vacancies. Although a sixteen-year period is covered, data are missing for some states in some years. The most complete data are for congressional and gubernatorial elections, which we tabulated from appropriate issues of the *Congressional Quarterly Weekly Report*. The *Congressional Quarterly Guide to U.S. Elections* (second edition) was also helpful.

In using these Congressional Quarterly publications, however, we opted not to incorporate their data on federal legislators and governors stretching back to the 1920s. As our subsequent analyses demonstrate, runoffs for high offices (election outcomes for lower offices are unavailable in the Congressional Quarterly publications) are frequently unlike the pattern more generally observed. We have attempted to avoid this high-office distortion by comparing a wider range of offices throughout the same period.

Through *Newsbank* (a microfiche collection of newspaper articles on elections across the country), we were able to find information on the race, gender, and other characteristics of some primary candidates. Unfortunately, this coverage is episodic and uneven in quality.

The determination of runoff frequencies for positions other than member of Congress and governor was achieved through an inspection of state election returns. Arkansas, Georgia, Florida, Louisiana, Mississippi, and Oklahoma do the best job of making these materials available through official channels. Texas state senate returns are readily available, but those for the house are not. Several states do not publicize their vote returns in primary elections; for these states—with the exception of Arkansas—it is difficult to obtain the data. Even a trip to the capitol of one of them was unavailing. Through professional contacts, however, we managed to obtain the election returns for some years in Alabama and South Carolina. We were never able to obtain data on legislative primaries in North Carolina.

Finally, as a supplement to this data set, we reanalyzed Ewing's raw figures for the years 1920–48 (obtained from the Western History Collection archives at the University of Oklahoma), applying more modern statistical methods than were available to him at the time. The Ewing data have the virtue of covering state legislative contests as well as higher offices.

Where appropriate in this book, we have incorporated materials from data sets in other studies. Specifically, we have drawn on the data set of Charles Bullock and Susan MacManus that analyzes certain aspects of municipal runoffs and on the data set of Bullock and A. Brock Smith that analyzes race and runoff elections for county offices in Georgia.[16] With these supplementary data, we are able to shed additional light on the fate of women and blacks in runoff elections.

In a number of the cities analyzed by Bullock and MacManus requiring a majority vote, the elections were nonpartisan; thus, no general election followed a primary (and potential runoff) as in the contests covered by our data set. However, there is a strong similarity between the majority-vote requirement in nonpartisan municipalities, on the one hand, and the requirement for a majority vote for nomination in much of the South, on the other hand. Traditionally, the Democratic nomination guaranteed success in the general election because the GOP did not field candidates. The same pattern prevailed in most southern counties and perhaps even in most legislative contests at the state level.

Indeed, Republicans continue to give some Democrats a bye even in congressional and statewide contests. In a growing number of suburban areas, however, the situation has been just the reverse, with the Democrats offering no competition to Republican nominees (such as in the case of some Cobb County offices in suburban Atlanta). Consequently, while southern states always have staged general elections, the great bulk of these during the last century have been pro forma. So although we acknowledge the potential for a difference in the runoff primary and the majority-vote general election in a nonpartisan city, in practice they are often similar.

Two dependent variables are preeminent in our analysis: (1) whether the candidate who led in the primary went on to win the runoff, and (2) the share of the vote garnered by the primary leader in the runoff. The specialist will want to note that the statistical technique of ordinary least squares regression has been used in this study to estimate models in which the share of the vote received by the primary leader in the runoff is the dependent variable. And because the other dependent variable—whether the primary leader won the runoff—is dichotomous, logit models have been employed. The generalist will be happy to know that we have tried to explain our findings in plain English as well.

The Frequency of Second Primaries

The first issue addressed is the incidence of the runoff primary. Under what conditions are runoffs likely to take place? Do runoffs occur with sufficient frequency to have a significant influence on leadership selection? Has the incidence of second primaries declined as two-party competition has risen in the South? Is their frequency related to the office being contested, with runoffs required more often for positions of high prestige? Is there much disparity in the frequency of runoffs among the states that hold them? And, finally, how widespread is the runoff requirement in America's cities?

Research Expectations

We hypothesized that the presence of an incumbent in the race would have a strong influence on the need for a runoff. More specifically, runoffs would be more frequent in open-seat contests. We suspected that the existence of an open seat would stir the ambitions of a number of credible candidates, producing a highly competitive field. The presence of several capable office seekers would work against the likelihood of any one candidate achieving a majority vote during the first balloting.

We expected, too, that the status of the office contested might affect the chances of a runoff primary. If the office is prestigious, such as that of governor or U.S. senator, it is likely to attract a larger number of prominent candidates than, obviously, the job of municipal dogcatcher or, more seriously, even the opportunity to serve in the U.S. House of Representatives. In the data analysis below, we examine the interplay between the effects of incumbency and the status of a given office. In some circumstances, the two reinforce the likelihood of increased runoffs, whereas in other circumstances the two variables work at cross-purposes.

The phenomenon of postcensus redistricting also drew our attention. For offices below the statewide level, redistricting can result in the placement of two incumbents within the same electoral boundaries, or it can so redraw an incumbent's territory that he or she loses the competitive edge of long-standing ties with a constituency. In the latter case, the once-safe officeholder may seek retirement rather than face the task of nurturing new relationships with a fresh set of voters. More likely, however, such a situation will produce more and stronger challengers.

Similarly, we would anticipate that robust two-party competition might discourage runoffs. In one-party regions, the fruits of public office are within the reach of only those candidates who compete in the nominating primary of the dominant party (for example, until recently, the Democratic party in the South). This situation produces competitiveness and, often, a bruising battle requiring a runoff. Though the eventual nominee may be battered as he or she enters the general election, the contest in a one-party environment is virtually over by then, as the weak (or nonexistent) opposition party is unable to field a serious candidate. In contrast, in two-party, competitive situations, a battered nominee stands to lose. Therefore, pressures are at work within each party to produce a strong, consensus candidate—one free, ideally, from the buffeting of rough-and-tumble first and second primaries.

The Data

Most of the data presented in this analysis of runoff frequency come from a review of primary elections held in the South from 1970 through 1986. We have collected data on contests for governorships, the U.S. Senate, and the U.S. House of Representatives.[17] The nomination process for each party for each office has been treated separately; thus, the data set consists of more than 1,900 observations. The full sixteen-year period is analyzed for nine of the states. Data for Louisiana in this section cover only 1970 through 1974. Beginning with elections in 1975, that state modified its primary system so that all candidates run in the same primary—regardless of party affiliation. Louisiana holds a runoff only when no candidate receives a majority.

The level of primary competition was coded in four categories: (1) there was no candidate—either the party failed to field a nominee or the nominee was chosen by a party convention rather than in a primary, (2) the primary was uncontested, (3) the primary was contested but one of the candidates won a majority in the first contest, and (4) after a competitive primary, a runoff was necessary to select the nominee.

The Findings: Runoffs Occur Often Enough to Matter

Almost 10 percent of the primaries required a runoff. Although this is the least frequent of the four categories reported in Table 1.2, it nonetheless accounts for a significant share of all contested elections. If one excludes the more than 250 instances where a party avoided a primary and situations where a single candidate sought the nomination, then fully a quarter of all *contested* primaries resulted in runoffs. When at least three candidates sought the nomination, the runoff was far from a rarity. Political scientists are chiefly interested in competitive elections; accordingly, only the 717 primaries that were contested would merit extensive study.

Runoffs by Type of Office

By definition, the occurrence of a runoff indicates heated competition. Nominations for more desirable offices should, therefore, be determined more frequently in a runoff than would be the case for less desirable positions. The higher the status associated with a position, the greater the likelihood that even long-shot candidates will run. With larger fields of candidates, it becomes less probable that one will poll a majority in the initial primary. This leads us to expect that runoffs will be less common for the U.S. House than for the other two positions analyzed. Governors and U.S. senators both have statewide constituencies; the former is, arguably, more prestigious than the latter, however, as each state has but a single governor.

As further evidence that the governorship is more desirable, some senators leave Washington to seek that office (recently, California Republican Pete

Table 1.2 Degree of Competition for Nomination, by Office, 1970–1986:
A Frequency Distribution (Number of Cases in Parentheses)

Office	No Candidate	Uncontested Primary	Contested Primary	Runoff	Total
Governorship	1.0%	17.0%	48.0%	34.0%	100.0%
	(1)	(17)	(48)	(34)	(100)
U.S. Senate	3.9	22.5	50.0	23.5	99.9
	(4)	(23)	(51)	(24)	(102)
U.S. House	14.8	51.7	26.4	7.1	100.0
	(247)	(865)	(442)	(118)	(1,672)
Total	13.5	48.3	28.9	9.4	100.1
	(252)	(905)	(541)	(176)	(1,874)

Wilson, for one). Governors may run for the Senate after completing their terms or, occasionally, conspire to have themselves named to fill a vacancy. Rarely, however, do governors run for the Senate when doing so would jeopardize their tenures in the statehouse. Further, during the period for which data were collected, the governorship proved to be a surer stepping stone than a Senate seat to a presidential nomination. The last person to move directly to the presidency from the Senate was John F. Kennedy (D-Mass.) in 1960. In the last two decades, George McGovern (D-S.Dak.) was the only sitting senator to be nominated for the presidency (1972) whereas there were five instances in which a party's nominee had recently served as governor.[18]

Prestigious Offices
As expected, our inquiries show that runoffs did become more common as the political status associated with a position increased. A third of the gubernatorial contests were decided in a runoff, compared with just under a quarter of the senatorial nominations. Further, Table 1.2 shows that runoffs for a seat in the House were relatively infrequent, accounting for fewer than 10 percent of all nominations.

A more complete exploration of Table 1.2 confirms that competitiveness increased with the status of the position. Fully 82 percent of the gubernatorial nominations involved a contested primary, and in all but one instance both parties fielded candidates. Approximately three-fourths of the senatorial primaries were contested, although in four cases the minority party had no Senate candidate. A third of the House nominations were contested, while 14.8 percent of the time one party offered no candidate. The time when a Democrat running for a top-of-the-ticket contest could go on vacation after securing a majority of the primary electorate is but a fond and fading memory for Democrats. Southern campaigns, particularly for governor and U.S. senator, like the region's Indian summer, now continue right into November.

Most House nominations go uncontested; indeed, contested primaries for these seats in states with the runoff rule have been less frequent recently than they were a generation ago. Harvey Schantz found that, nationally, 40 percent of the House primaries were contested between 1956 and 1974.[19] The decline in contested primaries in the runoff states may be related to Schantz's observation that primaries are least likely to be contested in safe Democratic districts held by an incumbent. As the number of secure offices in these districts declines, Schwartz predicts, there will be more frequent competition. To the extent that this is occurring, it may be further evidence that the South is becoming more like the rest of the nation politically.

Open Seats

Desirability may not be the only factor operating to determine the incidence of runoffs; a second element may be the absence of an incumbent. The well-recognized potency of incumbency tends to dissuade potentially strong challenges, particularly for less desirable posts.[20] During the early years of our study, most southern governors were prohibited from succeeding themselves, and even today most states in the region limit consecutive service to two terms. Therefore, at regular intervals the governor's office will be vacant. The disparity between competitiveness for governors and U.S. senators may be partially a product of incumbency. Southern senators have traditionally been a durable species, serving much longer than governors.

The absence of open seats probably goes a long way to explain the much lower levels of competition for the House. Contributing to the absence of

competition, especially instances where the minority party failed to put forward a candidate, may be the relatively small size of congressional districts.
A congressional district is more likely to have a homogeneous population than
the state,[21] so the opposition party may have less basis on which to build in a
congressional district than statewide. The short, two-year terms of House
members (which—except for the Arkansas governor prior to 1986—is shorter
than that of other positions analyzed here) forces incumbents to forge closer
ties with their constituents.[22] The smaller size of House districts also encourages representatives to embrace home styles that involve extensive personal
contact. Senators doubt whether personal contacts will pay off because they
can meet so small a share of their constituents.[23] In contrast, House members
believe that cultivation of the electoral garden back home helps keep in check
the bramble bush of opposition.

Competition across States

The degree of competition varied across the states that use a runoff rule.
Second primaries were required most often in Mississippi and in Oklahoma,
the one nonsouthern state to require a majority vote for nomination. As shown
in Table 1.3, if contested primaries and runoffs were combined, then Oklahoma would have been the most competitive state. Of states for which we
have extensive data, primaries were least common in North Carolina and
Texas, two of the four Rim South states. In both of these states, fewer than
7.5 percent of the nominations were decided in a runoff.

Steven Haeberle analyzed gubernatorial and senatorial nominations from
1932 to 1986.[24] He found that, among Democrats, gubernatorial nominations
were most often resolved in runoffs in Mississippi and Florida and senatorial
nominations went to runoffs most often in Oklahoma (35 percent of the time).
Haeberle's research, which includes an earlier period when more states limited governors to a single term, confirms some of our findings as to which
states are more likely to have runoffs.

In the uncompetitive category, the Deep South states exhibited a weak tendency to have the most frequently unchallenged general elections. In most of
these states, serious Republican challenges came at least a decade after those

Table 1.3 Degree of Competition for Nomination, by State, 1970–1986
(Number of Cases in Parentheses)

State	No Candidate	Uncontested Primary	Contested Primary	Runoff	Total
Alabama	15.1%	48.7%	26.3%	9.9%	100.0%
	(23)	(74)	(40)	(15)	(152)
Arkansas	17.0	50.0	24.0	9.0	100.0
	(17)	(50)	(24)	(9)	(100)
Florida	13.6	52.9	22.9	10.7	100.1
	(42)	(164)	(71)	(33)	(310)
Georgia	16.8	43.1	29.2	10.9	100.0
	(34)	(87)	(59)	(22)	(202)
Louisiana*	27.8	33.3	31.5	7.4	100.0
	(15)	(18)	(17)	(4)	(54)
Mississippi	16.4	46.4	24.6	12.7	100.0
	(18)	(51)	(27)	(14)	(110)
North Carolina	5.5	55.5	31.7	7.3	100.0
	(12)	(121)	(69)	(16)	(218)
Oklahoma	5.5	42.2	39.8	12.5	100.0
	(7)	(54)	(51)	(16)	(128)
South Carolina	7.8	57.0	24.2	10.9	100.1
	(10)	(73)	(31)	(14)	(128)
Texas	15.7	45.1	32.2	7.0	100.0
	(74)	(213)	(152)	(33)	(427)

*Louisiana data for 1970–74 only.

in the Rim South states. In Alabama, Georgia, and Mississippi, the minority party offered no candidate more than 15 percent of the time. The one Deep South state out of line with this tendency was South Carolina, where the general election was uncontested 8 percent of the time. Popular U.S. senator Strom Thurmond's conversion to the GOP in 1964 gave that party a jump start in the Palmetto State, unlike in other Deep South states where serious, indigenous Republicans emerged later and have been less formidable than Thurmond. Among the Rim South states, Arkansas and Texas had uncontested general elections as frequently as did three of the Deep South states (Alabama, Georgia, and Mississippi).

The high level of competition in Oklahoma is the most notable exception to the hypothesis that two-party competition will reduce intraparty competition, as Oklahoma has the longest history of two-party competition of any state included here. Oklahoma's frequent runoffs lend support to the claim that a majority-vote requirement encourages multicandidate fields.[25]

The higher incidence in the Deep South of the failure of one party to field a candidate, however, underscores the tenacity of one-party politics in that area. In that regard, Arkansas shares characteristics with the Deep South. Arkansas was the last southern state to vote for a Republican presidential nominee, not doing so until 1968. It also demonstrated its southern heritage when it gave a larger share of its 1976 vote to Jimmy Carter (65 percent) than did any other southern state except for his home state of Georgia (67 percent). Finally, as of 1991, Arkansas and Louisiana remained the only southern states never to have had a popularly elected Republican U.S. senator.

Frequency over Time

No clear pattern emerges for the incidence of runoffs over time.[26] The frequency of runoffs in 1984 and 1986, when almost 8 percent of the nominations were determined in a second primary, is about the same as in 1970 and 1974. There is no evidence in Table 1.4 that runoffs have declined as party competition has grown. Nor is there an oscillating cycle, with runoff incidence fluctuating in a predictable pattern from on year to off year. There is some indication, though, that runoffs—and primary competition generally— are linked to redistricting. Two of the three years with the most runoffs were 1972 and 1982, years when newly redrawn districts were first used for House elections.

No pattern emerges for the frequency with which one party failed to field a candidate. The highest number of uncontested general elections occurred in 1970: just under 19 percent. If we had gone further back in time, then certainly the number of instances where the GOP lacked a candidate would rise. The high percentage of no-candidate situations in 1970 may have marked the end of the era in which the Republican party was too weak even to offer token

Table 1.4 Degree of Competition for Nomination, by Year, 1970–1986
(Number of Cases in Parentheses)

Year	No Candidate	Uncontested Primary	Contested Primary	Runoff	Total
1970	18.6%	55.7%	19.0%	6.7%	100%
	(39)	(117)	(40)	(14)	(210)
1972	15.7	41.7	30.6	12.0	100
	(34)	(90)	(66)	(26)	(216)
1974	14.7	47.8	29.5	8.0	100
	(33)	(107)	(66)	(18)	(224)
1976	12.9	45.1	33.3	8.6	100
	(24)	(84)	(62)	(16)	(186)
1978	12.4	40.0	34.3	13.3	100
	(26)	(84)	(72)	(28)	(210)
1980	10.8	57.2	22.7	9.3	100
	(21)	(111)	(44)	(18)	(210)
1982	9.0	47.6	31.9	11.5	100
	(19)	(100)	(67)	(24)	(210)
1984	13.8	49.5	29.1	7.6	100
	(29)	(104)	(61)	(16)	(210)
1986	12.6	50.5	29.4	7.5	100
	(27)	(108)	(63)	(16)	(214)

Note: Mississippi and Louisiana gubernatorial elections have been combined with those held in other states in the previous offyear. Thus, 1970 and 1971 elections were combined.

candidates in much of the South. In recent years the frequency of uncontested general elections has fluctuated between 10 and 15 percent, with the 13.8 percent in 1984 being the highest in a decade. In 1982 the share of uncontested general elections (9 percent) was the lowest of any of the election years considered and may be partially attributable to the redistricting of House seats that year. A greater number of open seats and changes in the districts of incumbents probably convinced an inordinate number of aspirants that 1982 was an auspicious year to try their luck.

Party Competitiveness

Because runoff elections were adopted when the Democratic party was the only party in most of the South, it is not surprising that primary competitiveness generally is more prevalent in the Democratic party than in the Republican party. As suggested in Table 1.5, runoffs are three times more likely to occur among Democrats than Republicans. For just over half of all positions available from 1970 to 1986, at least two candidates ran in the Democratic primary. In contrast, for only one-fourth of the gubernatorial and congressional seats did two or more Republicans run.[27] At the other extreme, Democrats failed to field a candidate in less than 3 percent of all contests, whereas Republicans were without a candidate one-fourth of the time.

The data in Table 1.5 confirm the literature reporting that intraparty competition is more intense in the party likely to prevail in the general election. The record for southern nominations from 1970 to 1986 is similar to what Schantz found for the U.S. House from 1956 to 1974.[28] With Democrats always holding at least 60 percent of the House seats and most statewide and legislative offices, they clearly remain the dominant party in the South, despite recent slippage. Democratic dominance encourages a wide ideological range of candidates to compete for nominations within that party. The number and diversity of candidates in Democratic primaries accounts for the greater primary competition.

Haeberle's study of fifty-four years of gubernatorial and senatorial nominations also founds runoffs to be more a Democratic than a Republican phenomenon.[29] Between 1932 and 1986, in majority-vote states, 49.7 percent of the Democratic gubernatorial nominations and 18.4 percent of the senatorial nominations required a runoff; on the Republican side, the corresponding figures were 4.2 percent and 5.1 percent.

The Importance of Incumbency

The hope that surrounds an open seat generates far greater competition than when one must challenge an incumbent. As reported in Table 1.6, multiple candidates emerged in more than three-fourths of all primaries for open seats,

Table 1.5 Competitiveness, by Party, 1970–1986
(Number of Cases in Parentheses)

Party	No Candidate	Uncontested Primary	Contested Primary	Runoff	Total
Democratic	2.5%	46.0%	37.3%	14.3%	100.1%
	(23)	(431)	(349)	(134)	(937)
Republican	24.4	50.6	20.5	4.5	100.0
	(229)	(474)	(192)	(42)	(937)

and in 40.8 percent of the primaries to fill a vacancy, a runoff was necessary. In contrast, runoffs were held only 5 percent of the time when an incumbent was on the ballot.

Democrats versus Republicans
The traditional Democratic dominance in the South is still visible if we dis-aggregate the figures in Table 1.6. In only 3 percent of the instances where there was a Democratic incumbent did a runoff become necessary in either party. When there was a Republican incumbent, however, Democrats staged runoffs 16 percent of the time in their enthusiasm to regain what was prob-ably seen as rightfully a Democratic position (a GOP runoff occurred only 1 percent of the time when there was a Republican incumbent). Democrats infrequently (12 percent) allowed Republican incumbents to go unchallenged, whereas more than a third of the time (36 percent) Republicans fielded no opponent to a Democratic incumbent. GOP leaders have, at times, discour-aged their followers from mounting hopeless challenges to well-ensconced Democratic incumbents. The Republican rationale has been that a futile chal-lenge will nonetheless inspire the unbeatable Democrat to campaign aggres-sively, which may turn out voters who would otherwise sit out the election.[30] Once at the polls, the weakly identifying Democratic voters may swamp Re-publican candidates for other offices.

As the new party in the South, the GOP is less likely to have multiple candidates when it holds a seat. Indeed, we found that 86 percent of the time Republican incumbents faced no primary opposition. Democrats were less

Table 1.6 Incumbency and Runoff Frequency, 1970–1986
(Number of Cases in Parentheses)

	No Candidate	Uncontested Primary	Contested Primary	Runoff	Total
Open seat	3.1%	18.7%	37.4%	40.8%	100%
	(8)	(49)	(98)	(107)	(262)
Democratic incumbent	18.0	50.6	28.4	3.0	100
	(221)	(621)	(349)	(37)	(1,228)
GOP incumbent	6.0	61.2	24.5	8.3	100
	(23)	(235)	(94)	(32)	(384)

deferential to their incumbents, who were able to escape a primary challenge only 58 percent of the time. In half of the instances where a Republican incumbent was on the ballot, several Democrats competed for the opportunity to dislodge the officeholder. In contrast, Republicans hesitated to take on Democratic incumbents, with more than one Republican seeking the honor less than 21 percent of the time. As the traditional minority party, the GOP may have lacked a pool of quality candidates; the party may also have been reluctant to expend resources on low-probability challenges to Democratic incumbents, or it may have feared that a divisive primary could endanger the GOP's status as an emerging challenger for power.[31]

Republican nominees, then, usually entered the general election well rested, without having had to expend energy, money, or goodwill in a primary. They generally faced a Democrat who had already experienced at least one election campaign. It was this scenario that prompted Edwin Edwards, who had to survive a runoff on the way to the Louisiana governorship in 1971, to mount the effort to adopt the nonpartisan electoral format now used in his state. Democratic incumbents who have had to stave off an opponent in the primary should, all other things being equal, be more susceptible to a GOP challenger in the general election, as the Republican has probably not had to face a primary opponent. If the nomination stage within the Democratic party is too bitter, the rancor may persist in the general election campaign—again to the advantage of the GOP. As two Democratic gubernatorial nominees discovered in 1986, if the opponent from the runoff refuses to lend support, the nomination becomes worthless. The loser of the Florida Democratic gubernatorial runoff became a Republican and served in the administration of the Republican governor elected that year. In Alabama, the runoff did not pick the Democratic nominee. The runoff loser challenged the outcome, claiming that the winner, who was the sitting attorney general, had failed to enforce state law precluding Republicans from voting in the Democratic runoff. Indeed, the attorney general, himself a former Republican, had sought Republican backing in the runoff. A federal court invalidated the runoff results and the Democratic executive committee awarded the nomination to the loser of the runoff. The deposed Democratic nominee, after pondering a write-in campaign, swung his support to the Republican, an unknown who capitalized on the Democratic disarray to become Alabama's first GOP governor of this century.

Governors versus Legislators

Looking at individual offices, we found that runoffs decided the gubernatorial nominee half of the time when there was an open seat or when a Republican sought a second term. Only 10 percent of the time was there a runoff when a Democratic incumbent was seeking reelection. The nominees for open Senate seats were somewhat less likely to be chosen through runoffs (41 percent of the time). Democratic incumbency was more likely to be accompanied by a runoff for a Senate seat, however, than for a gubernatorial seat.

The incidence of runoffs for open House seats (38.4 percent) was on a par with that for open Senate seats. Competition for House seats that had an incumbent was substantially less than for other types of offices, regardless of whether the incumbent was a Democrat or a Republican. Fewer than 2 percent of the seats filled by Democrats had a runoff. The smallness of congressional districts and the assiduousness with which incumbents cater to their constituents make House members far less susceptible to defeat than are officials with statewide constituencies. Potential challengers are well aware of the rate at which House incumbents are turned out. Consequently, most House incumbents face minimal opposition.

Party Distinctions

The relative frequency of runoffs for open seats masked a partisan difference. For all three offices, runoffs were much more common in the Democratic than in the Republican party. When the governor's mansion was vacant, the Democratic nominee was five times more likely (84 percent of the time) to be chosen in a runoff than was the Republican nominee (16 percent). Democratic nominees for open Senate seats experienced runoffs almost two-thirds of the time, compared with 18 percent of the time for GOP nominees. And for open House seats, the Democratic nominee was selected through a runoff more than three times as often as the Republicans (58 percent to 16 percent).

Another pattern that persisted for all three offices was the higher rate of Democratic runoffs when there was a Republican incumbent than, conversely, for a runoff to choose a GOP challenger over a sitting Democrat. In four of five elections involving a Republican governor, the Democratic nominee was chosen in the runoff; only one of twenty Republican challengers to a sitting Democratic governor had to endure a runoff. The contrasts were less extreme for the Senate, where 25 percent of the Democratic challengers to Republican senators were named in a runoff, as opposed to 18 percent of the Republican challengers to Democratic senators. For the honor of taking on a member of the U.S. House, 13 percent of the Democratic challengers had a runoff before facing a sitting Republican; Republican opponents to Democratic incumbents, however, virtually never had runoffs (less than 2 percent of the time).

The data for individual states reveals that runoffs for open seats occurred between 25 and 50 percent of the time. They were least common in Arkansas and most common in Georgia. When there was a Republican incumbent, the range in runoffs extended from 3 percent to 15 percent, with runoffs least common in Texas and most frequent in Arkansas. (This comparison excludes Louisiana, which had only two contests involving an incumbent Republican.)

Majority-Vote Requirements for Cities

While only ten states have a runoff provision in the primary, numerous American cities use the runoff provision. A majority-vote requirement, along with at-large elections and nonpartisanship, was part of the Good Government reform movement initiated during the early part of the twentieth century. To the extent that nonpartisan elections were adopted, a system similar to that found in the American South was imposed. As long as the Democratic party remained dominant, the South experienced no partisan competition. Similarly, by erasing party lines and holding nonpartisan elections, many cities eliminated party competition.

In 1986 Susan MacManus conducted a survey of all American cities that had a population of at least 25,000 in 1980. Most of the 946 cities contacted had a runoff provision.

The Runoff Primary: A Central Feature of American Elections

Since its inception near the turn of the century, a majority-vote requirement has attained a position of prominence in U.S. elections. This is especially true in the South, a region long dominated by the Democratic party—whose nominating primaries have become tantamount to final elections; but it is true as well in municipalities across the land. Thus, despite neglect by scholars of electoral politics, the runoff is alive and well in the trenches of America's political campaigns.

The runoff procedure is particularly apt to surface in those state and city elections where several candidates face each other in a primary contest. In contested primaries, a runoff becomes necessary about one-fourth of the time. The incidence of runoffs is also related to the type of office being sought. They occur most frequently in races for the office of governor. For this political plum, but for all the other offices studied in this book as well, second primaries have been most common in those elections devoid of an incumbent seeking another term. Further, regardless of how many candidates are involved, the office sought, or whether an incumbent is on the ballot, runoffs are substantially more numerous in the Democratic party than in the GOP. Our results show some variation from state to state, but not much, and the patterns revealed in the data have persisted over time.

In terms of its frequency of usage alone, we believe that the runoff primary warrants closer attention than it has received by students of politics and the general public. Its significance, however, extends far beyond the arid (though revealing) statistics on frequency. Despite its relative obscurity as a subject of serious analysis, the runoff has managed to become a topic of widespread controversy—from the lofty perches of the Justice Department in Washington, D.C., to the lower courts and political precincts of the rural South. Over the years it has also generated a number of myths, to which we now turn.

2 Myths of the Runoff

Four major myths have grown up around the runoff procedure. At the core of each lies a criticism that calls seriously into question the equity of this electoral method, namely, that the second primary yields different nominees than would a single primary based on plurality voting. In contrast, friends of the runoff point to the lower probability of the Condorcet Paradox occurring under the second-primary system. For them, the justification of the runoff lies in the likelihood that it will produce the candidate with the widest base of support, as opposed to the outcome of a plurality system when multiple candidates seek office.

For reasons that will become apparent, we give to these four myths—by which we mean popular folk or commonly accepted wisdom—the following labels: the *leader-loses myth*, the *incumbent-loses myth*, the *female-loses myth*, and the *minority-loses myth*. In this chapter, we examine the first three myths in depth and then set the stage for an extended discussion of the fourth and most controversial myth—the issue of minority disadvantage—in chapters 3 and 4.

The First Three Myths: Perceptions

The Leader-Loses Myth

A sense has developed, especially among politicians and media pundits, that the candidates who tally the highest number of votes in the initial primary are doomed to defeat in the runoff. The reason for this, according to one version of the conventional wisdom, is that voters tend to be sympathetic to the underdog—Number 2 in the first primary—and rally behind his or her candidacy. This behavior is common in sports. For example, during the 1988 Olympics in Seoul, fans cheered for the women of Peru as they combated the women of the mighty Soviet Union for a gold medal in volleyball. Had the outcome of this game been determined by balloting in the stands, Peru would have gone home with the gold.

One election watcher has referred to the supposed advantage of trailing in the opening primary as the "mystique of second place."[1] This notion has been reinforced by a number of prominent come-from-behind victories for Democrats in recent years. In Florida, Senator Lawton M. Chiles, Senator D. Robert Graham, and Governor Reubin O. Askew all achieved victory by leapfrogging from second place to overcome the primary front-runner in the runoff and then going on to win the general election. In Alabama, in 1970, the legendary George C. Wallace came from behind in the primary (he had placed second among three candidates for governor) to defeat Albert Brewer by 33,881 votes in the runoff. In Arkansas, in 1954, another well-known southern politician, Orval E. Faubus, who would soon inflame passions by blocking black students from Little Rock's Central High School, overcame a primary ballot deficit of almost 14 percent (45,265 votes) to nip Francis Cherry in the runoff for the governorship by 1.8 percent of the total vote. In another of several examples, in a Georgia race for U.S. senator in 1972, Sam Nunn—now widely viewed as one of the nation's top authorities on defense issues—overcame a distant second-place showing in the primary (among fifteen candidates) to defeat incumbent David H. Gambrell in the runoff.

Being Number 2 has allowed some underdogs to portray themselves as struggling reformers pitted against powerful establishment candidates, a David against Goliath. In 1988 Congressman Kenneth H. ("Buddy") MacKay used to advantage his second-place finish in the initial primary to fill the seat vacated by retiring Senator Chiles. His opponent, Bill Gunter, garnered 38 percent of the first-primary vote yet lost the runoff in October with 48 percent of the vote. The leapfrog myth took another jump forward.

When Democrat Ray Mabus won the runoff after leading in the initial primary in 1987, he became the first Mississippi governor to triumph in both contests in twenty-four years. In all five gubernatorial primaries from 1967 to 1983, a runoff was needed to determine the next governor, and in each of these the primary front-runner stumbled and fell in the runoff.

In a less visible vote—yet one well covered in the Atlanta newspapers—a twenty-four-year-old second-place finisher in the initial vote for an Atlanta City Council seat, Jared L. Samples, went on to defeat incumbent Archie Byron by a 214-vote margin in a 1988 runoff. Both candidates were black. Byron had done well in the opening contest, narrowly missing an outright majority of the vote. Then Samples gathered in 54.9 percent of the vote in the second primary (actually tabulating slightly fewer votes than he had in the first election). In contrast, Byron plummeted by more than 2,600 votes— evidently, his overconfident initial supporters had stayed home for the second vote. Samples became the youngest council member since voters chose a twenty-three-year-old in 1983. This leader-loses result captured the newspaper headlines, even though all the other first-election leaders won their runoffs in Atlanta.[2]

The statistics on election outcomes contradict the widespread notion that to place is better than to win in the first primary. In Florida, more telling than the MacKay upset is the fact that, before Gunter, no Democratic senatorial candidate in this century who received more than 33 percent of the vote in the opening primary had gone on to lose.[3] The MacKay and the Samples victories should be seen as statistical outliers, risky for use as benchmarks to predict future runoff results.

The leader-loses myth is so pervasive that some politicians even see front-runner status as a handicap if it fails to deliver a first-primary majority. Former Georgia labor commissioner Sam Caldwell writes about the 1966 Georgia Democratic gubernatorial primary: "Jimmy Gray [one of the candidates] knew if he could come in second to [former governor Ellis] Arnall in the primary, he had an excellent chance of winning the runoff." Caldwell describes the scene after Arnall was pushed into a runoff against runner-up Lester Maddox (Gray finished a distant fourth): "The handwriting was on the wall, and nobody knew it better than Arnall. He had been the frontrunner for so long that he almost had to win without a runoff. Now, he was going into the runoff with little chance to increase the margin he had in the primary by enough votes to win." Commenting on the likelihood that the primary leader will stumble in the runoff, James Foster observed: "It's very common. If you take 100 races at random, the smartest bet would be on the second-place finisher."[4]

Former Georgia governor Carl Sanders explains the ability of the runner-up to capture ultimate victory in terms of America's infatuation with the underdog: "Psychologically, the person who comes in first initially finds himself the overwhelming favorite to win office. He's now the frontrunner. What often follows is a tendency for the voters to want to help the guy who came in second, whom they perceive to be as good as the guy who came in first. It's not so much that the other candidates gang up on the frontrunner, as it is the voters turning toward the underdog."[5] Sympathy for the underdog as a potent voting cue is most likely when there are few differences on issues between the candidates.[6] Support for the underdog or a playful desire to upset the plans of the candidate touted as front-runner going into the initial primary may have been a powerful voting cue in the issueless, personality campaigns that were frequent in the traditionally one-party South.

Of course, interstate differences may exist. A. J. Liebling described a bargaining process in Louisiana in which candidates eliminated in the first primary negotiated with the survivors for considerations in the next administration. Benefits included patronage positions, government contracts, and favorable legislation. While Liebling believed that the losers usually united against the front-runner, he said of the market for endorsements: "Naturally, the runoff candidate who looks more likely to win can buy support at lower political prices than any other fellow, but by trying to drive too hard a bargain he may send the business to the underdog. Many a man has beaten himself that way."[7]

Cortez A. M. Ewing also alluded to negotiations between the agents of the surviving and the eliminated candidates, a process in which "[s]trange liaisons are made." V. O. Key, Jr., commented on postprimary bargaining for support from those who failed to make the runoff. He noted a tendency for the first gubernatorial primary to be cluttered with numerous minor candidates; these candidates then supported the runoff participant, who assumed responsibility for their campaign debts.[8]

Thus, the runoff feature could be an incentive for marginal candidates to compete, knowing that they had little to lose; if they were eliminated in the first primary, a "sugar daddy" would cover their expenses.

Based on cases like the ones presented above, the considered wisdom of politicians and those who watch them is that leading the primary field, rather than boding well for the runoff, has been a prelude to disaster. The precarious position of the front-runner may result from public sympathy for the runner-up; the jealousy of those eliminated, who then empathize with the second-place finisher rather than the candidate who outpolled all others; or more astute negotiating by the runner-up, who secures the endorsements of the more popular individuals eliminated in the primary.

Merle and Earl Black see in the defeat of primary front-runners a valuable means of strengthening the Democratic party.[9] They argue that primary front-runners who lose are typically politicians past their prime. The primary leader is often a former officeholder who loses the runoff to a hard-charging new face. The past record of these fading practitioners provides a sufficient base for them to win a plurality; by raising the ante and forcing them to obtain a majority, the Democratic party can avoid being saddled with nominees whose baggage includes a large number of opponents. Runoffs help eliminate candidates with what pollsters call "high negatives," that is, a large share of the public who prefers anyone to this particular candidate—a form of political natural selection in the Darwinian sense.

The Incumbent-Loses Myth

The second myth—equally suspect, we believe, and seemingly as widely held as the first—advances the idea that an incumbent must either win the opening primary or lose the nomination. If he or she stumbles at the first-primary stage, this "wound" will signal a fatal weakness. Given all the advantages of incumbency—from name recognition to the congressional franking privilege, PAC-preference, and other perks of office—any incumbent unable to coast across the finish line in first place must have failed badly as a public official, according to this perspective, and is now reaping the wrath of dissatisfied constituents. When this proposition was tested, the findings produced some surprising results.

For perspectives on the incumbent-loses myth, we turn again to politicians. When he was lieutenant governor of Georgia, Zell Miller (now governor) once asserted: "If an incumbent can't get 50 percent or more of the vote in the primary, my sense is that he's doomed." [10] Surprisingly, Miller made this statement four years after veteran Senator Herman Talmadge (1957–81) was held to less than a majority in the primary but nevertheless beat Miller by a three-to-two margin in a runoff for the 1980 senatorial nomination. The incumbent-loses myth is so strong that Miller continued to articulate it even after personally confronting contrary evidence. Perhaps Miller was thinking about Peter Zack Geer who, in 1966, as the lieutenant governor, proved unable to convert a 49.5 percent plurality into a runoff majority.

Miller's senatorial opponent in 1980 also recognized how widespread the incumbent-loses myth had become. In reviewing the events surrounding this (his last) campaign, Talmadge writes: "Since I was the central issue in this campaign, a lot of folks assumed that the candidates eliminated in the first primary would rally around my opponent in the runoff to present a united anti-Talmadge front. So when I got 42 percent of the vote in the first primary the pundits started writing my political obituary. To them that primary meant only one thing—that well over half of the Democrats in Georgia wanted Herman Talmadge out of the Senate." [11] In the runoff, Talmadge gathered 58.6 percent of the vote.

A less extreme view was offered by Melba Williams, Georgia's Democratic national committeewoman: "If an incumbent loses the first primary, he or she is in big trouble and is unlikely to win the runoff." Ewing, who studied runoffs that occurred between 1920 and 1948, agreed with Williams: "The odds are great indeed against an incumbent who cannot lead in the first race." [12]

The logic behind the key assumption of the incumbent-loses myth derives from the advantages with which incumbents enter campaigns. Incumbents are almost always better known than their challengers and this leg up should propel them to a plurality in a multicandidate field, even if their hold on the constituency is weakening. [13] Consider data from the 1980–84 congressional elections. Members of the U.S. House of Representatives enjoyed a huge advantage over challengers in name recognition. More than 90 percent of the respondents in the University of Michigan Survey Research Center samples recognized and could rate incumbents, compared with only 54–62 percent who were that familiar with the challengers. [14] The gap in recognition advantage for Senate incumbents over challengers, while smaller, was ten to twenty percentage points.

Given the tremendous advantages with which incumbents begin (and usually end) campaigns, it is small wonder that observers would conclude that incumbents forced into runoffs were fatally flawed. For an incumbent to be in a runoff, there must have been at least two challengers. Given the infrequency with which an incumbent attracts even a single serious challenger (see chapter 1), those who confront multiple opponents clearly have something about them that others perceive as vulnerable. In the initial primary, the approach may be that of the field against the incumbent.[15] Certainly this phenomenon characterizes some of the more visible recent contests forcing well-known incumbents into runoffs. In the 1980 Georgia Democratic senatorial primary, for example, three serious challengers and several minor ones took on four-term senator Herman Talmadge. The serious challengers concentrated more on explaining how they would improve on the incumbent's performance than on challenging one another's qualifications.

The strategic significance of ganging up on an incumbent was recognized by another Georgia politician, who advised: "Never run against an incumbent in a statewide race without at least three candidates on the ballot."[16] A field of this size, of course, has the potential of forcing a runoff and allowing one challenger to overcome a first-primary deficit.

Sam Caldwell speculates about the problems that incumbents face in runoffs for lesser statewide offices. He sees the incumbent attracting the votes of many people who have weakly held preferences in the first primary but who then pass up the runoff:

> The race for governor, lieutenant governor, or U.S. Senate receives almost all the publicity, and most of the voters go to the polls to cast their ballots in these races. Many of them are not usually interested in the races for . . . the various other so-called secondary races. Without any personal interest in the race, they will vote for the incumbent. But in a runoff, the circumstances are reversed. Usually only those voters interested in that particular race will go back to the polls to vote. . . . The runoff then becomes widely publicized, the challenger gains momentum, the voters find a reason to vote against the incumbent and decide it is time for a change.[17]

Although Caldwell's explanation is directed toward the secondary offices, there are doubtless some people who vote for top-of-the-ticket positions in the first primary solely on the basis of incumbency. These voters, who may have gone to the polls to support a neighbor for sheriff or county commissioner, may not bother to vote in the runoff. The moral seems to be that the various steps incumbents take to promote name identification will attract support, but the support obtained in this fashion is subject to substantial erosion.

Yet another perspective comes from the Blacks' study of gubernatorial runoffs. A relatively inexperienced challenger who can force a current or former incumbent into a runoff may gain credibility. According to the Blacks, "Managing to survive the first primary is often perceived as a breakthrough in mass support, a prelude to victory in the runoff." [18]

The importance attached to surviving a primary, for the challenger, is reinforced by research reported on congressional elections. Having pushed the incumbent to a one-on-one confrontation, the challenger should obtain greater media coverage than during the initial primary. Moreover, survival to a runoff may rejuvenate the challenger's fund-raising efforts. Holding the incumbent to less than half the vote may provide the challenger with the credibility needed to attract more contributions. Either the purchase of more ads or heightened media attention should promote the challenger's name recognition among voters so that challenger visibility to the electorate comes closer to equaling that of the incumbent. We know from congressional research that only challengers who are about as well known as incumbents stand much chance of victory. [19] A prolonged campaign does little to increase the name recognition of the incumbent, who is already widely known, but it may be critical to evening the odds for the challenger.

The Female-Loses Myth

Rev. Jesse Jackson has claimed that women are just as disadvantaged by the runoff provision as black candidates. If this were true, one would expect to find female front-runners in first primaries losing more often in the runoffs than male front-runners. On the road to testing the possibility of gender bias (as we discovered, yet another myth distorting the reality of the runoff provision), we considered several potential reasons for the development of the female-loses myth. Subscribers to the myth may believe that voters turn against female candidates in the second contest, concluding—however un-fairly—that women have inadequate temperament or training to cope with the pressures of high office. Gender and the status of the office sought could, in this sense, be interrelated: the higher the office, the less likely voters will turn to female candidates. Further, voters may oppose policy positions often as-sociated with women or with the feminist movement.

Money could also stand as a barrier to a woman's electoral success under the dual-primary system. In political campaigns, female candidates have often had to rely on volunteer workers rather than "fat cat" contributors (who are usually well-to-do white, middle-aged men).[20] Moreover, one would surmise that mobilizing volunteers for a second round of hard work could be difficult for a candidate (man or woman) who failed to show a strong chance of win-ning—though a woman who unexpectedly came close to beating her chief male rival in the first primary might actually inspire her campaign workers to redouble their efforts in the runoff.

Time might be a key variable as well. As the years march forward, the status of female political candidacies in the United States seems to be improv-ing; at any rate, more and more women are being elected to state and local offices. Indeed, for the first time two women serve in the U.S. Senate who were elected in their own right rather than simply taking over the seat of a deceased husband. In light of this increasing public support for women in office, it appears that the runoff has been less of a barrier in recent years than in the past.

The First Two Myths: Findings

The Primary Leader and the Runoff

The most controversial feature of the runoff primary is the potential it holds for a result that is different from that produced by a single-primary, plurality system. How widespread is the reversal of candidate order in the runoff? Our data reveal that the primary leader won the runoff 70 percent of the time. While the runoff frequently produced results different from the primary, it is clear that the leader-loses myth is a serious overstatement.

Although certainly not supporting the leader-loses myth, Table 2.1 does reveal some variation across offices in the success rates of primary leaders. The primary leaders most susceptible to defeat were U.S. Senate and gubernatorial candidates; they managed to win runoffs little more than half the time. Primary leaders running for lieutenant governor also did relatively poorly, with only eight of thirteen holding onto a win. Aside from these three top-of-the-ticket offices, there was little variation in the success rates of other primary leaders. For other posts, primary leaders won at least 70 percent of the time; the most successful group included candidates for various secondary statewide offices other than lieutenant governor,[21] who held off challenges in the runoff almost three-fourths of the time.

The results in Table 2.1 are similar to those obtained from an analysis of Georgia runoffs from 1965 to 1982. Sixty-eight percent of the primary leaders in Georgia won runoffs, with the least successful candidates being gubernatorial aspirants.[22] Three of Georgia's last four governors finished second in the initial primary and then overtook the front-runner in the second primary; Jimmy Carter was the single exception—grist for the leader-loses mill.

The Blacks report that between 1966 and 1986, 53 percent of the Democratic gubernatorial front-runners were nominated. Their figure is similar to what we found, but our findings are somewhat lower than they report for the 1920 to 1965 period. During the earlier period, gubernatorial front-runners were nominated 63 percent of the time, which is almost identical to the figure reported by Key for the thirty years ending in 1948.[23]

A study of runoffs in the city council contests for Dallas, Fort Worth, and San Antonio, Texas, provides figures that are similar to those for all offices included in Table 2.1. In runoffs for seventy-five at-large municipal seats, the primary front-runner won 72 percent of the time.[24] The 66 percent success rate for front-runners seeking seats in single-member districts is also within the general range that we observed for state and federal positions.

The relatively low success rates for governors and senators may be the basis for the leader-loses myth. When people think of runoffs, they are likely to recall the most visible contests. The attention accorded gubernatorial and senatorial elections by the media, especially if accompanied by solemn pro-

Table 2.1 Success Rate of Primary Leaders in Runoffs, by Office, 1970–1986

Office	Primary Leaders		
	Won	Lost	N
Governor	56.3%	43.8%	32
Lt. Governor	61.5	38.5	13
Other statewide executive offices	73.3	26.7	30
U.S. Senator	54.2	45.8	24
U.S. House	71.4	28.6	112
State Senate	72.0	28.0	225
State House	70.4	29.6	786
Total	70.1	30.0	1,222

nouncements of the leader-loses myth, may stick in the minds of both politicians and average citizens.

Two loose ends need to be tied up. First, why were lesser statewide officials more successful than gubernatorial and senatorial front-runners? The infrequency with which the lower-office candidates lost runoffs may derive from the more limited visibility of positions such as secretary of state and attorney general. The relative dearth of public attention focused on these offices may have removed a critical element in rallying support behind the runner-up during the second primary. The high success rate for statewide executive officials (other than the governor or lieutenant governor) refutes the leader-loses view put forward by Sam Caldwell.

Second, why were leading candidates for the state senate and state house triumphant in runoffs at nearly identical rates? The implication of the earlier discussion is that because house districts are generally smaller than senate districts, front-runners should be more successful in lower-chamber contests. The explanation may be that differences in the size of state house and senate districts are not so great as to produce different amounts and types of contact between candidates and constituents.[25]

State Differences

Our data show some variation among states in the rate at which primary front-runners win second primaries. Plurality leaders were least successful in North Carolina, where only half of the primary leaders won nomination (see Table 2.2). At the other extreme, more than 70 percent of the primary front-runners in Alabama, Arkansas, and Florida went on to victory in the runoff. Two of the three states where a primary plurality least often identified the nominee are states for which we were unable to obtain comprehensive data on state legislative contests: North Carolina and South Carolina.[26] Thus, the data sets for the Carolinas disproportionately comprise statistics on gubernatorial and senatorial elections, in which, as Table 2.1 shows, primary front-runners enjoyed the lowest number of runoff victories.

A Longitudinal Perspective

After reviewing three rounds of runoffs in Louisiana, Stella Theodoulou observes that the frequency with which the primary leader loses has been increasing.[27] Rising vulnerability is not, however, the pattern for the states surveyed in this study. Table 2.3 reports relatively little variation in the success rates of primary front-runners over time. These rates range from 65 percent to 78 percent. To the extent that there is a pattern, it differs from what Theodoulou found in Louisiana. Indeed, from 1983 to 1986, 74 percent of the primary leaders were nominated—the highest success rate for any three consecutive election years in our data set.

Table 2.3 reveals some decline in the number of runoffs. The greatest number of dual primaries were held in 1974 and 1978, when there were more than 150 a year. Offices that were filled in those two years would also be contested in 1982 and 1986. A 15 percent decline in runoffs occurred between 1978 and 1982; by 1986 there were only 62 percent as many runoffs as eight years earlier. The figures for 1975, 1979, and 1983 come from Louisiana and Mississippi, which hold state elections in off years. Again there was about a 40 percent drop in the number of runoffs between 1975 and the latter two years.

This decline in the number of heavily contested nominations might have resulted from the growing Republican challenge. As the GOP becomes a vi-

Table 2.2 Success Rate of Primary Leaders in Runoffs, by State, 1970–1986

State	Primary Leaders		
	Won	Lost	N
Alabama	74.1%	25.9%	166
Arkansas	73.6	26.4	87
Florida	72.7	27.4	234
Georgia	68.8	31.2	215
Louisiana	69.8	30.2	116
Mississippi	68.7	31.3	150
North Carolina	50.0	50.0	20
Oklahoma	66.7	33.3	150
South Carolina	66.7	33.3	45
Texas	69.2	30.8	39

able competitor in the South, we can anticipate the presence of fewer Democratic candidates, in part because some of the more conservative aspirants will run as Republicans. In the past, when Republicans had no hope of success, the entire ideological spectrum competed within the Democratic party. With the Democrats no longer having to accommodate all serious candidates and the entire electorate, it is likely that inconclusive first primaries will become less common.

The decline in the number of runoffs over time for this data set is at variance with the frequency of runoffs discussed in chapter 1. Recall that in the first chapter, our discussion was limited to congressional and gubernatorial elections. The longitudinal decline reported here is a product of fewer runoffs occurring for the less visible offices. The great bulk of the positions considered here are in the state legislature. Because these officials came from relatively small constituencies, we would expect that they more often represented one-party areas than did the incumbents of the offices analyzed in chapter 1. Therefore, a decline in the number of Democratic candidates in reaction to GOP growth applies less to the data reviewed here than it does to our findings in chapter 1.

Table 2.3 Success Rate of Primary Leaders
in Runoffs over Time, 1970–1986

| | Primary Leaders | | |
Year	Won	Lost	N
1970–71	67.2%	32.8%	58
1972	65.8	34.2	120
1974	72.1	27.9	154
1975	72.6	27.4	113
1976	66.4	33.6	107
1978	71.1	28.9	159
1979	66.7	33.3	66
1980	66.2	33.8	68
1982	68.7	31.3	134
1983	72.2	27.8	72
1984	77.3	22.7	75
1986	72.9	27.1	96

An alternative to the GOP-emerging hypothesis that might account for the drop in the number of runoffs would focus on challenger quality to explain the reduction in the number of serious candidacies. Incumbent invincibility among members of the U.S. House reached record levels in 1986 and 1988, culminating a trend toward fewer competitive districts that started in the mid-1960s.[28] More skillful use of the perquisites of office, the erosion of partisan ties, and the daunting need for larger sums of campaign money, which seems to have frightened away potentially viable challengers to House members, may also be discouraging some who, in the past, would have run for the state legislature.

Another factor that could explain the decline in the number of seriously contested state legislative elections is the spread of careerism among state lawmakers. Whereas an open seat has a magnetic effect on the ambitious politician, the prospect of facing a popular incumbent paralyzes many prospective challengers. A decline in voluntary retirements means fewer open seats, and with fewer open seats there are fewer multicandidate contests. As multicandidate contests become less common, runoffs are less often necessary.

First-Primary Strength

We anticipate that candidates who have run particularly well in the first primary are more likely ultimately to be nominated. Two measures are used to assess front-runner strength in the primary. The first of these is the percentage difference in the vote of the primary front-runner and the runner-up. The second is the "40-plus-5" measure suggested by Black and Black.[29] In their study of gubernatorial runoffs, the Blacks found that gubernatorial primary leaders are particularly likely to be nominated if they have at least a five-percentage-point lead over the second-place finisher and if they received at least 40 percent of the total vote.

An examination of the correlation coefficients between the two measures of the primary leader's strength and whether that person is nominated shows that the first measure (the margin between the front-runner and the runner-up) is more strongly related to runoff success. The correlation coefficient for the first measure is .27, whereas for the Blacks' measure the correlation is .18. A similar pattern prevails when the share of the vote in the runoff going to the primary leader is correlated with the two measures of primary strength. Again, the correlation is greater with the difference in the primary leader's margin ($r = .32$) than with the Blacks' measure ($r = .20$).

When we dichotomized our contests using the Blacks' 40-plus-5 rule, we observed greater success among primary leaders who met the two components of the rule. Eighty percent of the primary leaders who turned in strong initial performances were nominated, contrasted with a nomination rate of 63 percent for candidates who had less convincing primary showings. Figures compiled by the Blacks for gubernatorial runoffs between 1920 and 1986 reveal even more pronounced differences, with 87.5 percent of the strong front-runners being nominated compared with 53 percent of the weaker performers. The Blacks' research shows that the impact of the initial primary performance has become more pronounced in recent years, with all 40-plus-5 gubernatorial leaders since 1966 winning their second primaries.[30]

Size of Primary Field

Table 2.4 reports the relationship between the size of the primary field and the ultimate success of the primary leader. Primary leaders were most likely to win nomination when they came from moderate-sized fields of four, five, or seven candidates. They were least successful when the initial field had eight or more contenders. In large candidate fields the vote is widely dispersed. If no candidate has a commanding lead in the first primary, and if many of the initial contestants are eliminated, the possible coalitions that can produce a runoff winner are numerous.

Although Table 2.4 suggests that large primary fields made the job of the primary leader particularly difficult, the pattern is similar to what we found in our earlier study of the Georgia runoffs.[31] For neither a dichotomous variable of win/lose nor the percentage of the runoff vote taken by the primary leader is there a significant correlation with the size of the primary fields. Indeed, for both measures the correlation is slightly negative and for neither does the coefficient ever reach a puny .03.

Table 2.4 also shows that almost half of all the runoffs analyzed had initial fields of three candidates. Three-and four- candidate fields accounted for almost three-fourths of the elections that went into runoffs. Only one in seven runoffs followed an initial contest with six or more candidates.

Impact of Party

Almost 90 percent of our runoffs took place in the Democratic party, despite increasing GOP competition. There was, however, no meaningful difference between the parties in the rate of success for first-primary leaders.

Comparison with Ewing's Data

We are able to make some comparisons between our data for the post–1970 era and the data collected by Cortez Ewing for the period 1920 through

Table 2.4 Number of First-Primary Candidates and Success Rate
of Primary Leaders in Runoffs, 1970–1986

| | Primary Leaders | | |
Number of Candidates	Won	Lost	N
3	68.8%	31.2%	554
4	73.2	26.8	336
5	72.2	27.9	158
6	66.7	33.3	93
7	73.8	26.2	42
8	55.0	45.0	20
9–15	57.9	42.1	19

1948.[32] For the most part, we will report on an analysis of 188 runoffs for the same kinds of offices that we have analyzed for the recent period. With a few exceptions, we do not rely on the full set of 492 runoffs on which Ewing gathered information, as he included judicial and local contests, as well as contests for some multimember administrative bodies, all of which are outside the scope of this study.

The rate at which primary leaders won runoffs in Ewing's study is slightly higher than for comparable offices in the more recent era. Almost 72 percent of the primary leaders were nominated. A review of all 464 Democratic runoffs on which Ewing gathered information shows greater leader dominance, with the primary leader winning 73.1 percent of the nominations. Ewing's figures are so similar to ours that we are confident that the leader-loses myth was no more accurate in the past than it is today. Indeed, if anything, the leader-loses myth was even less appropriate for earlier generations. That statement applies not only to the statewide contests covered in this book but also to local elections. In a set of 116 local contests surveyed by Ewing, the primary leader was nominated 75 percent of the time. This success rate is slightly higher than that reported by Arnold Fleischmann and Lana Stein in their study of local contests in three Texas cities.[33]

The success rate of primary leaders has varied with the office being contested. Ewing's results parallel ours to the extent that leaders in contests for governor and lieutenant governor were among the least successful in maintaining an original lead. Table 2.5 shows that in the gubernatorial elections studied by Ewing, the primary leader won 58 percent of the nominations, compared with 56 percent in our data set. The primary leader for the position of lieutenant governor was nominated 64 percent of the time in Ewing's era, as opposed to 61.5 percent of the time in ours. The most striking difference is in the high level of success (77 percent) for leaders in U.S. Senate primaries during the Ewing period. This rate is about 50 percent higher than we observed (54 percent). Success levels for U.S. House leaders are also somewhat higher than we observed. The figures for state legislators are very close to what we reported.[34]

Ewing's figures show a much greater range in primary leader success across states than we found (see Table 2.6). At the low end were South Carolina and Arkansas, where only about 56 percent of the primary leaders were nominated. In sharp contrast, primary leaders in North Carolina were nominated 95 percent of the time. Because we do not know what offices were included for each state in Ewing's complete data set, as reported in the right-hand columns of Table 2.6, we cannot determine whether his distribution of offices is different from ours. For the set of comparable offices, for which figures are given in the left-hand columns of Table 2.6, only four states have a sufficient number of cases to allow a comparison. The figures from Florida and Texas are similar for the two time periods, whereas North Carolina and Oklahoma primary leaders won more runoffs in the earlier period.

Because of the limited number of cases in Ewing's study, we analyzed his data by decade instead of by year. The results revealed variations, with primary leaders being most successful during the 1930s and least successful during the next decade. The relatively high incidence of leader losses during the 1940s was not attributable to the post–World War II demobilization. We had thought that perhaps the GI revolution, such as Key described for Arkansas, would have shown up with an inordinate number of people finishing second in the primary but then subsequently winning nomination.[35] Although leaders did lose about 32 percent of their runoffs in 1946, that figure was

Table 2.5 Success Rate of Primary Leaders in Runoffs, by Office, 1920–1948

Office	Primary Leaders		
	Won	Lost	N
Governor	57.9%	42.1%	19
Lt. Governor	64.3	35.7	14
Other statewide executive offices	68.6	31.4	24
U.S. Senate	76.9	23.1	13
U.S. House	76.0	24.0	75
State Legislature	72.7	27.3	22
Total	71.8	28.2	188

Source: Cortez A. M. Ewing, *Primary Elections in the South: A Study in Uniparty Politics* (Norman: University of Oklahoma Press, 1953).

exceeded by leader losses of approximately 43 percent in both 1940 and 1942—well before the political activities of World War II veterans.

An early single-state study provides further evidence that the leader-loses myth was no more an accurate portrayal of reality in the past than it is today. A review of a wide range of 1944 Arkansas elections at all levels turned up 48 runoffs, 73 percent of which were won by the primary leader.[36] In keeping with Ewing's findings, candidates for Arkansas judgeships were particularly susceptible to having an initial plurality overturned—a fate that befell six of eleven primary leaders for the bench. The leaders' rate of success in Arkansas half a century ago echoed the results of a more extensive study reported in 1940, in which 76 percent of the plurality leaders won nomination.[37]

Ewing's data show that front-runners who had given a strong performance in the primary, applying the standard set out by the Blacks,[38] were more advantaged in earlier generations than they would be today. Of the individuals who met the 40-plus-5 threshold, 91 percent were nominated. This figure is 11 points higher than we observed and even exceeds the Blacks' results for gubernatorial runoffs held between 1920 and 1986. The

Table 2.6 Success Rate of Primary Leaders in Runoffs, by State, 1920–1948

State	Offices Comparable to Post–1970 Data		All Ewing Elections	
	%	N	%	N
Alabama	—	—	76.4	55
Arkansas	60.0	5	55.6	9
Florida	70.5	44	72.6	73
Louisiana	—	—	59.4	32
Mississippi	61.5	13	70.8	89
North Carolina	100.0	19	95.2	21
Oklahoma	82.5	40	80.2	81
South Carolina	—	—	55.6	20
Texas	68.7	67	72.6	84
Total			73.1	464

Source: Figures in the "All Ewing Elections" column are from Cortez A. M. Ewing, *Primary Elections in the South: A Study in Uniparty Politics* (Norman: University of Oklahoma Press, 1953), p. 97. They are only for Democratic runoffs; twenty-eight GOP runoffs are not included in Ewing's tabular presentation.

momentum of a strong first-primary showing seems generally to have been greater in the past than more recently, despite the Blacks' contrary findings for gubernatorial elections. Among primary leaders who had less impressive initial showings, the success rate (64.1) was only 1.5 points higher than in the current era.

Incumbency and the Runoff

Based on the data we gathered on runoffs from 1970 to 1986, it appears that the incumbent-loses myth has also been overstated (see Table 2.7). Although incumbents forced into runoffs are more vulnerable than primary leaders in contests without incumbents, in our study incumbent front-runners won 64.7 percent of the time. In runoffs between two nonincumbents, the primary

Table 2.7 Success Rate of Primary Leaders in Runoffs,
Controlling for Incumbency, 1970–1986

| | Primary Leaders | | |
	Won	Lost	N
No incumbent	71.6%	28.4%	830
Incumbent present	66.8	33.2	364*
Incumbent led primary	64.7	35.3	272
Incumbent second in primary	73.6	26.4	91

*The number of runoffs in which an incumbent participated (364) exceeded by one
the sum for the two subcategories because in one runoff following a redistricting,
both candidates were incumbents.
Note: We were unable to determine incumbency status for 28 of the runoffs.

leader won 71.6 percent of the time. Only in cases where incumbents trailed
after the first primary were runoffs extraordinarily dangerous to their longev-
ity. Of ninety-one incumbents who entered a runoff as the underdog, only
twenty-four survived.

Table 2.7 suggests that incumbent front-runners do experience somewhat
greater problems than other primary leaders, although clearly incumbents
who win pluralities have a strong probability of being reelected. In our study,
the difference in the likelihood of an incumbent winning a runoff after leading
the primary was approximately seven percentage points less than that of the
primary leader for an open seat and nine points less than that of a challenger
who bested the incumbent in the first primary.

Fleischmann and Stein's analysis of success rates for primary front-runners
in three Texas cities (Dallas, Fort Worth, and San Antonio) also controls for
incumbency. In at-large contests, incumbents who had led the first primary
defeated nonincumbents two-thirds of the time, while nonincumbents who
won a plurality in the first primary defeated incumbents in the runoff 64 percent of the time. Though the number of cases is small, a different picture
emerged in contests for single-member district seats, where front-running
incumbents won only two out of six nominations against challengers in con-

trast with six out of seven front-running challengers who took seats from incumbents. Front-running Texas municipal incumbents campaigning at large were as likely to win runoffs as the front-running incumbents in our data set. The success rate of the few incumbents running in districts was much lower than the 65.6 percent success rate of front-runners generally seeking single-member districts. Caution is appropriate in interpreting the Texas data for districted incumbents, given their small number.[39]

Although our set of incumbents was not greatly disadvantaged, the perquisites associated with officeholding did not consistently help an incumbent who had been bested by a challenger in the first heat. Richard Fenno warns against viewing incumbency as a suit of armor donned by all officeholders.[40] Incumbents who finish second in a primary may be those who failed to maximize the opportunities available to them. Based on Table 2.7, the real surprise is not that these incumbents lost (for their rate of defeat is about the same as that for second-place finishers in open-seat contests), but that they finished second in the initial primary.

Perhaps the incumbent-loses myth draws its support from the success rates of *all* incumbents faced with runoffs. When all incumbents competing in second primaries are considered, only 55.8 percent won renomination. The renomination rate for incumbents in runoffs pales beside that for all incumbents who sought additional terms. Even incumbents who received a first-primary plurality were only two-thirds as likely to be reelected as were all incumbent members of the U.S. House and state legislators who sought additional terms.[41] Moreover, incumbents won runoffs less often than did leading candidates running for open seats. However, runoffs are *not* inherently fatal to incumbents.

We infer from Table 2.7 that incumbents are forced into runoffs relatively infrequently. Although we lack counts of the frequency with which incumbents seek reelection to the types of offices included in our study, we suspect that the proportion exceeds 75 percent. In contrast, only about 30 percent of the runoffs in our study involved incumbents. Therefore, though some incumbents draw potent opposition, most do not. The great bulk of the runoffs occur in open-seat contests, which we expect will generally attract larger sets of serious candidates.[42]

Incumbency and Office

A review of incumbent runoff losses by office sheds light on the basis for the incumbent-loses myth. Most susceptible, as shown in Table 2.8, are those who hold the highest offices. As with the leader-loses myth, the incumbent-loses myth draws its greatest support from top-of-the-ticket positions. Among the most visible contests, only two of six incumbent U.S. senators who led their primaries held on to win nomination, a fate shared by one of two incumbent governors who led a primary but were forced into runoffs. Five of eight members of the U.S. House who led the primary won renomination, as did almost two-thirds of the state legislators.

All of the few statewide officeholders and the U.S. House incumbents who placed second in the primary lost the runoff. Legislators who finished second in the primary were more successful, winning come-from-behind victories more than a quarter of the time.

The Constituency-Contact Hypothesis

A potential explanation for the greater vulnerability of incumbents pursuing renomination to higher offices is the variation in the extent of personal contact between voter and candidate. Elected leaders who represent smaller constituencies should be able, all other things being equal, to have multiple kinds of contact with a larger share of their constituents than can politicians with more populous constituencies. A growing literature has demonstrated that voters are more likely to support candidates with whom they have had contact.[43] During any given period, statewide candidates personally encounter a smaller proportion of their constituents than do candidates for the state legislature.

The longer terms of gubernatorial and senatorial offices create fewer incentives for contact than exist for holders of other offices. U.S. senators must be rechartered by their electorates every six years, and all governorships included in this study, except that for Arkansas, held four-year terms.[44] All state house members, except those in Louisiana and Mississippi, and U.S. representatives and most state senators must face the voters biennially. Incumbents serving two-year terms are continuously campaigning, whereas longer terms allow incumbent senators and governors to tend the constituency garden less assidu-

Table 2.8 Success Rate of Incumbents in Runoffs, by Office, 1970–1986
(Number of Cases in Parentheses)

Office	Incumbents' Finish in Primary	
	First	Second
Statewide	54.5%	0%
	(11)	(3)
U.S. House	62.5	0
	(8)	(2)
State Senate	66.1	30.4
	(56)	(23)
State House	65.0	27.0
	(197)	(63)

ously. Thus, the higher failure rate for statewide incumbents may stem from a combination of their losing touch with constituents and the greater visibility of their positions.

One perspective on variations in the attention accorded constituents can be gleaned from evidence on the frequency with which legislators return to their districts. A review of the travel records of one southern senator disclosed a sharp rise in the number of days spent in his state during reelection years and an even more precipitous drop immediately following reelection.[45] Most members of the U.S. House make regular (often weekly) trips to their districts, which are largely unaffected by the imminence of an election or by seniority.[46] Because their responsibilities are defined as part-time, southern state legislators live and work in their districts for most of the year; this promotes more extensive contact with constituents than that undertaken by incumbents of the other offices included in this study.

Another manifestation of constituency concern is provided by variations in the roll-call voting of legislators. In his study of California state legislators, James Kuklinski found that members of the lower chamber did not vary during the course of their two-year terms in the degree to which they voted in accordance with the policy preferences of their constituents. In contrast, California senators, who have four-year terms, distanced themselves from their constituents' preferences in the aftermath of an election and then brought their roll-call voting behavior more into line with these preferences as election day approached. Richard Elling has shown a weak pattern of oscillation in the voting behavior of U.S. senators, who take more moderate stands in the years in which they stand for reelection than in other years.[47]

To summarize, time in the district among the voters and the weight accorded perceived constituent preferences are most constant for incumbents who represent smaller constituencies and vary during the period of service for officeholders with longer terms. Consistency in policy stands, along with more frequent and more widespread contact with constituents, may explain why more runoff victories go to incumbents who are farther down the ticket.

The incumbents' low levels of success in runoffs for statewide office may stem from the scope of their constituency, that is, the population of the geographic entity represented by an incumbent. A state legislator, if rebuked by the electorate, can, through an aggressive campaign, personally contact a larger portion of the voters than can a statewide official. By seeking the forgiveness of voters, demonstrating renewed zeal, asking for support, or using some other ploy, more than a quarter of the state legislators reversed an unfavorable initial result. To achieve such a turnaround between the first and second primaries may require a more personalized appeal than is feasible for candidates contesting a larger constituency, who invariably lose after an initial second-place finish.

State Differences

In our study, the ability of incumbents to convert pluralities into runoff majorities varied substantially across states (see Table 2.9). Alabama incumbents were most successful, going on to win nominations after leading in the primary 81 percent of the time; in sharp contrast, front-running incumbents in Georgia won nomination less than half the time. Incumbents who led the primary were also notably unsuccessful in Florida and South Carolina; in both states, incumbents won nomination less than 60 percent of the time.

The states in which front-running incumbents were least successful are in

Table 2.9 Success Rate of Incumbents in Runoffs, by State, 1970–1986
(Number of Cases in Parentheses)

	Incumbents' Finish in Primary	
State	First	Second
Alabama	81.4%	60.0%
	(43)	(15)
Arkansas	66.7	16.7
	(18)	(6)
Florida	59.3	25.0
	(27)	(8)
Georgia	47.6	20.0
	(63)	(20)
Louisiana	70.3	10.0
	(37)	(10)
Mississippi	69.1	26.3
	(55)	(19)
North Carolina	*	*
Oklahoma	68.4	0.0
	(19)	(6)
South Carolina	57.1	40.0
	(7)	(5)
Texas	*	*

*Four or fewer cases per category.

the Southeast; two (Florida and Georgia) are among the more rapidly developing states (there were too few cases in Texas, another growth state, for us to place any weight on the data for that state). Incumbents who led the primary won renomination at higher rates in slower-growing states such as Alabama, Louisiana, and Mississippi. Incumbents in states that are experiencing slower growth may be advantaged if a larger share of their voters have had positive attitudes toward the officeholder in previous elections based on various aspects of constituency service. In states where in-migration has been greater, incumbents may have a smaller reservoir of good feelings to draw upon because of greater changes in the makeup of their constituencies and, consequently, lose runoffs more often.

Election Cycles

There is a relationship between election cycles and the success of incumbents forced into runoffs. The first pattern to be extracted from Table 2.10 is that incumbents who led primaries in 1975, 1979, and 1983 were successful 70 percent of the time. (Only Mississippi and Louisiana scheduled elections on this cycle.) This contrasts with a 62 percent success rate for front-running incumbents in other years, most of whom, except for congressional candidates, were running in states other than Louisiana and Mississippi. The second pattern is for plurality incumbents to be least successful in presidential election years. For the presidential years from 1972 to 1984, only 57 percent of the incumbents who led primaries won renomination. The success of incumbents who were first in the primary in off years (1970, 1974, and so forth) fell between that for incumbents running in presidential years and those running in off-off years (1975, 1979, and 1983). (State elections that occur neither in an off year nor in a presidential year we dub "off-off-year" cycles.) Thus, the more divorced elections are from presidential elections, the more likely that incumbents who placed first in the initial primary will be renominated.

The great bulk of the incumbents participating in dual primaries served in a state legislature. The implication from Table 2.10 is that these occupants of relatively low-visibility positions survived runoff scares best when they were most removed from the swirling crosscurrents of national politics. The explanation behind the pattern is far from clear. One possibility is that challengers to incumbents in presidential years are more likely to be quality candidates who have had officeholding experience and who are more proficient at raising campaign funds. A second possibility is that the security of incumbents is linked to turnout. Whereas *general election* participation rates tend to peak in presidential years, *primary election* turnout is often keyed to excitement about top-of-the-ticket contests.

Except in Arkansas and North Carolina, the governorship and other major

Table 2.10 Success Rate of Incumbents in Runoffs, by Election Cycle, 1970–1986 (Number of Cases in Parentheses)

| | Incumbents' Finish in Primary | |
Year	First	Second
1970	50.0%	33.3%
	(12)	(3)
1972	60.7	40.0
	(28)	(5)
1974	58.6	37.5
	(29)	(8)
1975	71.4	25.0
	(42)	(12)
1976	53.9	33.3
	(26)	(9)
1978	64.0	20.0
	(25)	(10)
1979	68.2	27.3
	(22)	(11)
1980	53.3	0
	(15)	(4)
1982	84.4	75.0
	(32)	(8)
1983	70.4	0
	(27)	(6)
1984	60.0	9.1
	(10)	(11)
1986	25.0	0
	(4)	(4)
1972, 1976, 1980, and 1984	57.0	20.7
(presidential years)	(79)	(29)
1970, 1974, 1978, 1982, and 1986	65.7	36.4
(off years)	(102)	(33)
1975, 1979, and 1983	70.3	20.7
(off-off years)	(91)	(29)

state offices are not chosen in presidential election years. In presidential years in most states, senatorial and congressional contests will be the top items on the primary ticket. Because tenure for governors, unlike that for members of Congress, is limited, state offices are more likely to be open than are congressional posts and thus stimulate more competition. Higher turnout in nonpresidential-year primaries brings a less politically active, less aware, and more volatile set of voters to the polls. When voting for state legislative candidates, these less-informed voters may often rely on cues—such as name recognition—that favor incumbents. (It is the performance of state legislative incumbents that largely determines the patterns shown in Table 2.10.) The smaller electorates that become involved in presidential-year primaries, where the ballot is usually headed by members of Congress who rarely face serious opposition, may be less deferential to incumbency in those instances in which state legislators meet stiff challenges.

First-Primary Strength

Incumbents who ran well according to the Blacks' 40-plus-5 rule won the runoff 76 percent of the time. In contrast, only 52 percent of the incumbents who led the runoff but did not demonstrate strength according to the Blacks' standard were nominated. A strong showing in the initial primary was also critical for incumbents to succeed in the second election. Among incumbents who ran second in the initial primary, 30 percent bounced back to win nomination when they trailed by less than 5 percent in the first primary and their opponent was held to under 40 percent of the vote. When the challenger was strong in the first primary, only 18 percent of the incumbents were reprieved by the runoff.

Comparison with Ewing's Data

Ewing found that Democratic incumbents who led first primaries were re-nominated at the same rate that we observed. However, incumbents who placed second in the initial primary were more disadvantaged in the Ewing era than in ours.[48] The rate at which incumbents who were runners-up were nominated after 1970 (26 percent) is twice the rate discerned by Ewing

(13 percent). The disparity is at least partially a result of Ewing's having included a wider range of positions than we studied. None of his judicial incumbents who placed second were nominated. However, even among legislative and administrative incumbents, only 15 percent were able to overcome a second-place finish.

One surprising result from the Ewing study concerns the relationship between level of office and success of front-running incumbents. Ewing's data show that the more prestigious the office, the more likely that an incumbent who led the primary would be renominated. Among statewide incumbents, 82 percent converted a plurality to renominations, compared with 57 percent of those seeking intermediate offices and only half of the local candidates. Our results, as reported in Table 2.8 above, show statewide incumbents to be particularly unsuccessful in second primaries. Perhaps the less sophisticated media available at the time of Ewing's study made it more difficult for statewide challengers to communicate their names and appeal to a geographically scattered electorate. This might explain their lower success rates before the age of mass media.

Multivariate Analysis

We conducted multivariate analyses on our 1970–86 data to determine the more important correlates of success in runoff elections. Two measures of success were used. The first is whether the primary leader was nominated in the runoff. The second measure concentrates on the share of the vote received by the primary leader in the second election. Because the dependent variable—winning or losing—is dichotomous, logit is used when attempting to model nomination success. And because share of the vote is an interval measure, multiple regression is used for those models. Numerous models were estimated for each dependent variable but, to conserve space, only predictors that were significant at the .1 level or better are reported.

The logit model for front-runner success appears in Table 2.11. This table includes three strong predictors and three others that were significant at the .1 level. Far and away the best predictor was the size of the margin enjoyed by the front-runner in the primary. Front-runners also were more likely to be

Table 2.11 Logit Model for Front-runner Success in Runoffs

Variable	Coefficient	Standard Error	Chi Square
Intercept	−.048		
Primary margin	11.305	1.241	82.99
Statewide office	−.386	.233	2.74
Alabama	.493	.210	5.50
Arkansas	.502	.279	3.23
Off-off year	.300	.175	2.95
Incumbent	−.367	.146	6.32

Model chi square = 111.45

Correctly predicted = 70.0%

nominated when they ran in Alabama or Arkansas. Candidates for state offices in Louisiana and Mississippi were somewhat advantaged over other candidates, as shown by the off-off year term.

Front-runners for statewide offices did somewhat less well in runoffs, as had been predicted from the bivariate results reported in Table 2.1. Also, as anticipated, front-runners in primaries involving incumbents did less well than front-runners for open seats. When a primary involved an incumbent, the incumbent was three times as likely to be the front-runner; therefore, the negative coefficient indicates that incumbents did less well than front-runners for open seats. Although we have identified variables that are related to front-runner success, the overall performance of the model is unimpressive. The model correctly predicted 70.0 percent of the cases; however, a prediction that the front-runner would always win would be accurate 69.9 percent of the time. (See Table 2.12.)

Only two predictors met the .1 threshold for inclusion in the multiple regression model for the share of the vote won by the front-runner in the second primary. The larger the difference between the vote for the front-runner and the runner-up, the more likely that the initial leader would be nominated.

Table 2.12 Multiple Regression Model for
Share of Vote Won by Primary Leaders

Variable	Coefficient	Standard Error
Intercept	.504	
Primary margin	.408	.033
Incumbent	−.011	.005
R^2	.11	

Table 2.12 also shows that the presence of an incumbent reduced the share of
the vote for the front-runner. The model is able to account for about one-ninth
of the variance in vote share received by the primary front-runner.

These more advanced statistical methods reinforce some of the earlier findings. Primary leaders usually did better in runoffs when they had a solid lead
in the initial contest and if they were seeking an open seat.

Debunking the First Two Myths

Based on the findings of this study, the two myths examined thus far in this chapter are certainly overdrawn, if not wholly inaccurate. We found that, rather
than being a likely loser in the runoff, the primary front-runner won nomination almost 70 percent of the time. Moreover, voters nominated the front-
runner in almost 72 percent of the contests surveyed by Ewing. Only for the
top positions examined—governor, lieutenant governor, and U.S. senator—
were a large share of primary leaders defeated. For all other offices, 70 percent or more of the front-runners won. Even for the U.S. Senate, the position
for which primary leaders were least advantaged, most were nominated in the
second primary. In no state and in no year were most primary leaders defeated
in the runoff. Proponents of the leader-loses myth evidently focus on a few
highly contested and visible elections in which prominent front-runners failed
to survive the second faceoff. Although these instances are the exception, they
appear to constitute the wellspring of the leader-loses myth.

Our findings also provide no substantiation for the incumbent-loses myth.

Incumbents who led in primaries were renominated almost two-thirds of the time. Again, it was only in statewide contests that an incumbent was notably disadvantaged; and, even there, half of the incumbents survived after an initial lead. Only in 1986, based on a mere four cases, were front-running incumbents more likely to lose than win renomination.

Gender and the Second Primary

A key assumption behind the claim that runoffs impede the ability of women to win public office is that a woman may be able to gain a plurality in the first primary when two or more men oppose her. When she moves on to the second primary against a single opponent, however, the eliminated male candidates will rally to the side of the remaining man, carrying their supporters in the electorate with them in a triumph of *Kinder, Kirche, Kuche* tradition. In the past, when turnout rates for men exceeded those for women, it was readily assumed that men would unite behind their brothers to keep women from winning public office. More recently, though, turnout among women frequently exceeds that among men, so the assumption must now be that enough women will turn their backs on a sister to ensure her defeat by a combination of male and female votes.[49]

Eleanor Smeal, former president of the National Organization of Women (NOW), has been an outspoken critic of second primaries. In an analysis of eight runoffs involving women, Smeal found that women led six of the initial primaries only to lose the runoffs. In the other two contests, the female candidate who placed second initially won the runoff but lost in the general election. Smeal's data came from five congressional districts, one U.S. Senate primary, and two Mississippi gubernatorial primaries in the 1970s and early 1980s. These results led her to conclude that runoff primaries were of "no help to women."[50] Given the timing of her charge, Smeal may well have been alerted to the possibility of an inherent gender disadvantage in the runoff by Jesse Jackson's similar criticism on racial grounds, expressed shortly before.

Kenneth Spaulding, a black state legislator who was in the forefront of a movement to reduce North Carolina's threshold for party nominations from

50 to 40 percent, criticized the majority-vote requirement for creating "a systematic disincentive for political parties to deprive this state of . . . female and minority leadership."[51] Spaulding's efforts found favor with the North Carolina League of Women Voters, which supported reducing the share of the vote required for nomination. In some other states, however, the league has declined to criticize the runoff; in Georgia, this issue received detailed scrutiny in 1990.

Regardless of whether the effect of the double primary is similar for black and female candidates, attempts by black critics to enlist women in their cause is a politically astute means of expanding the antirunoff coalition. Blacks by themselves remain a minority in the United States; united with women of all races in an attack against alleged electoral discrimination, their numbers grow mighty.

This coalition strategy has, however, a central flaw: many women reject the Smeal position. Some female candidates who have won runoffs see the second primary as helpful. They believe that the second primary conveys to some voters who had initially discounted their bid for office a message that their campaign is serious—that they have a real chance to win. By surviving the first winnowing, according to this view, female contenders can attract votes from a portion of the electorate that heretofore assumed that a woman had no opportunity for victory. Voters who may have preferred to see a woman elected, or who preferred a particular female candidate but questioned the viability of her candidacy, will be encouraged by her initial win and rally to her cause in the runoff.

A Look at the Evidence on Women and Runoffs

The data used to evaluate the woman-loses myth come from two sources. The first source is a survey of the 946 American cities with populations over 25,000 to ascertain the gender of council members serving in early 1986.[52] The findings of this survey have allowed us to determine whether the incidence of female councillors is related to the presence of a majority-vote requirement. If Smeal is accurate, women should hold a smaller share of the council seats in cities having the requirement. Our second source is the data set used throughout this volume, that is, the 1,222 runoffs held for legislative and executive positions at the state and federal levels of government. A study of this empirical record offers insights into whether women are less likely than comparably situated men to win second primaries.

Runoffs and Female City Councillors

In the mid-1980s, there was little difference in the proportion of female council members in cities using a majority-vote or plurality rule for nomination. According to a 1991 study by Charles Bullock and Susan MacManus, summarized in Table 2.13, 18 percent of the council members in the majority-vote cities were female, compared with 20 percent in cities where a plurality was sufficient. This two-percentage-point difference is modest and is not duplicated when the data are considered by region. In the South and the West, there was no difference in the frequency with which women were elected to council positions under the two types of vote requirements. Northeastern cities requiring a majority vote were actually more likely to have women on their councils than were cities where a plurality sufficed. Only in the Midwest did more women serve on councils chosen by a plurality rule. The six-percentage-point difference in the Midwest accounts for the two-point national difference. Thus, the most that can be said—based on Table 2.13—is that, in the Midwest, female candidates for city council are disadvantaged when a majority vote is required; in the remainder of the country, however, the double primary seems to raise no barriers to service by women on the councils of America's larger cities.

Bullock and MacManus report only on officeholding; they do not address the question of whether female candidates faced stiffer obstacles than their male competitors in light of a potential second primary. The comparative success of female and male candidates in the runoff (the major concern here) has been explored in three Texas cities. Using data from Dallas, Fort Worth, and San Antonio from 1951 to 1985, Fleischmann and Stein report that six out of seven women who led first primaries seeking at-large seats, and three of four seeking district seats, went on to win the second primary.[53] This 82 percent success rate for women exceeded the success rates of all primary

Table 2.13 Average Percentage of Female Council Members,
by Region and Vote Requirement

	Vote Requirement	
Region	Majority Vote	Plurality
Midwest	17%	23%
Northeast	14	12
South	17	17
West	22	22
Nationwide	18	20

Source: Charles S. Bullock III and Susan A. MacManus "Municipal Electoral
Structure in the Election of Councilwomen," *Journal of Politics* 53 (February 1991):
76–89, based on data from a 1986 survey.

front-runners—72 percent in at-large contests and 66 percent in district contests. The advantages of being the front-runner are not tied to gender, as males
who won pluralities defeated their female opponents seven out of nine times
running at large and in four out of seven district contests. In the absence of a
majority-vote requirement, eleven women won pluralities and would have
been elected. The second chance provided by the runoff resulted in the election of fourteen women. Although the numbers of cases are obviously small,
they show no disadvantage for women in these Texas municipalities.

Gender and Runoff Success for Higher Office

None of the states in this study provided comprehensive identification of
women candidates; therefore, we classified as female those who had typically
feminine first names. This approach holds the risk that persons with a feminine first name could have been male—for example, the Beverly Lakes who
sought office in North Carolina. Conversely, we may have also misclassified
some women who had typically masculine first names. Of course, where we
knew the gender of the candidate, we used that information rather than simply

relying on the first names. Thus, Connie Mack, a Republican representative from Florida, and the two Beverly Lakes were correctly identified as male. The first names of candidates were unavailable in approximately one hundred runoffs; these are excluded from this analysis of gender and the runoff.

As stated earlier, from 1970 to 1986 approximately one-third of the primary front-runners lost in the runoff. In assessing whether the runoff is a disadvantage to women, this overall incidence of defeat for the primary leader serves as a benchmark. If female front-runners were unsuccessful at rates substantially greater than one-third, that result would support the Smeal accusation. A second way in which to assess the consequences of second primaries for women is to compare the success rate of female front-runners with that of men who led a primary and faced a woman in the runoff. If female front-runners did substantially worse than male front-runners who competed against a woman in the runoff, that result would also back up the Smeal proposition.

Order and Strength of Finish

In male-female runoffs, the front-runner—regardless of gender—won 78 percent of the time, a rate of success almost eight points greater than for the full data set. Although primary leaders were more often nominated in male-female than all-male runoffs, the success rates varied depending on whether a woman or a man led the initial vote. As shown in Table 2.14, female primary leaders won the runoff 72 percent of the time, whereas male candidates who led a woman in the first primary were nominated 83 percent of the time. Despite the greater success of men who faced women in a runoff, women were more likely to beat men than were men to defeat other men (a 67 percent success rate). In an earlier study, we observed that women faced no disadvantage when forced into a second primary.[54]

To better understand the dynamics of runoffs between women and men, and to compare patterns in these runoffs with all runoffs surveyed in this study, we turn to a set of variables introduced earlier in this chapter. They include the relative strength demonstrated by the plurality leader, the office being contested, the party, and the year of the election.

Women who had led the first primary by at least five percentage points, and who polled more than 40 percent of the vote (the Blacks' measure of primary

Table 2.14 Gender and the Incidence of Nomination
of Primary Leaders, 1970–1986

	Primary Leaders		
Gender	Won	Lost	N
All male	67.3%	32.7%	945
Female vs. male	77.7	22.2	166
Female led primary	72.2	27.9	79
Male led primary	82.8	17.3	87
All female	100.0	0	3

strength),[55] won nomination 86 percent of the time (see Table 2.15). Women who had led the primary, but less impressively, were nominated 61 percent of the time. Controlling for the strength shown by a man who had led the primary, we found some—but not much—difference in the rate at which women overcame the initial disadvantage. Of the women who were less than five percentage points behind the leader, or who faced a man who had received less than 40 percent of the vote in the initial primary, 19.6 percent were nominated, as compared with 13.5 percent of the women who had placed second to men who demonstrated greater initial strength. Table 2.15 shows no gender-based difference in the success rates of candidates with strong primary performances.

The figures in Table 2.15 suggest that a woman only infrequently attracts enough additional support after a second-place primary finish to win the runoff. Thus, the observation of some women that their performance in the first primary gave them expanded credibility is generally valid only for female front-runners. Although women with relatively modest primary leads were not nearly as successful as comparable men, or as women who had strong primary leads, the 61 percent success rate for women with modest primary leads is in line with the overall success rate for all primary front-runners with less impressive first-round leads, 63 percent of whom were nominated.

Table 2.15 Rate at Which Front-runners Were Nominated, Controlling for
Gender of Primary Leaders, 1970–1986 (Number of Cases in Parentheses)

| | Primary Lead | |
Gender	Strong*	Weak
Female led primary	85.7%	61.4%
	(35)	(44)
Male led primary	86.5	80.0
	(37)	(50)

*A strong lead in the primary occurred when the front-runner received at least 40
percent of all votes and 5 percent more of the vote than the second-place finisher.

Steeper Slopes near the Top

Despite the small number of cases, the available evidence suggests that
women continue to be disadvantaged when seeking higher offices. In our
study, of women running statewide, only two out of seven who had led in the
primary won nomination; among congressional candidates, five out of eight
women went on from a first-place primary finish to win nomination. In contrast, women running for the state legislature converted first-primary leads
into nominations more than three-quarters of the time. Table 2.16 further
shows that, except in two U.S. House elections and one state senate contest,
only in the lowest office considered—that is, the state house—did women
overcome a second-place finish in the initial primary.

Rising Success Rates

We anticipated that the success rate of women would increase over time, and
Table 2.17 does reveal an improvement for female front-runners in the dual-
primary system. During the 1970s, female primary leaders won nominations
less than two-thirds of the time; in the 1980s, their success rate eclipsed
80 percent, which approximated the success rate of male front-runners in the
first primary. Although female leaders did better in the 1980s, women who
placed second in the primary were less fortunate. As shown in Table 2.17,
the rate at which women overcame a second-place finish in the first primary
was slightly lower in the later time period.

Table 2.16 Success Rate of Women in Runoffs, Controlling for Primary
Finish and Level of Office, 1970–1986 (Number of Cases in Parentheses)

| | Success Rate of Women Who Finished | |
Office	First	Second
Statewide	28.6%	0%
	(7)	(7)
U.S. House	62.5	50.0
	(8)	(4)
State Senate	90.0	10.0
	(10)	(10)
State House	75.9	18.2
	(54)	(66)
Total number	79	87

To the extent that some voters in the past were unwilling to see women hold high public office, that attitude seems to have become less of an impediment for female front-runners. Recall, however, that the success rate for female front-runners even during the 1970s equaled that for the front-runners in all-male runoffs. Therefore, although women's chances improved in the 1980s, their earlier performances were hardly poor. Perhaps the fifteen-point rise in the success rate of female candidates resulted from the increased levels of political participation by women generally. All other things being equal, women may rally around a female candidate—particularly when she had done well in the first primary; thus, more women voters will produce more women nominees.

Party Differences

Women in Democratic primaries have had an advantage over women in Republican primaries. As shown in Table 2.18, both first- and second-place female finishers were more likely to be nominated if they were Democrats—although the difference is trivial for women who ran second. The greater success enjoyed by Democratic front-runners may be attributable to the widely publicized "gender gap" that has worked to the advantage of the

Table 2.17 Success Rate of Women in Runoffs over Time
(Number of Cases in Parentheses)

	1970–1979	1980–1986
Female led first primary	62.5%	82.1%
	(40)	(39)
Male led first primary	18.2	15.6
	(55)	(32)

last several Democratic presidential candidates. With women more likely than men to vote Democratic in general elections, women may constitute a larger share of the electorate in Democratic than in GOP primaries. Or Democrats—being somewhat more liberal—may have a larger share of nontraditionalists in their electorate who are willing to see women in public office.

Multivariate Analysis

This section presents a multivariate analysis of circumstances identified in the preceding pages as potentially important to an understanding of female success in runoff primaries. As demonstrated above, women who placed first in a primary were overwhelming favorites to win nomination, whereas their sisters who ran second had little likelihood of a runoff triumph. Further, women who ran for state legislative offices were more successful than those seeking higher positions, and front-running women in the 1980s did better than those in the 1970s.[56] The other variables included in the models below are a measure of the disparity between the primary leader and the runner-up and a dummy variable indicating whether the primary was Republican or Democratic. A regression model is estimated using as a dependent variable the share of the vote won in the runoff by the female candidate. Also tested is a logit model in which the dependent variable is whether the woman won the primary.

In both models reported in Table 2.19, the order of finish is statistically significant. The negative sign for those coefficients indicates that women who led in the initial primary went on to win the runoff. The logit model shows that women seeking state legislative seats were more successful than women

Table 2.18 Success Rate of Women in Runoffs, by Party
(Number of Cases in Parentheses)

| | Success Rate of Women Who Finished | |
Party	First	Second
Democratic	73.9%	17.7%
	(65)	(68)
Republican	64.3	15.8
	(14)	(19)

who ran for higher offices. No other variable comes close to being statistically significant.

The regression model for share of the vote won by the woman in the runoff explains almost a third of the variance. Although the logit model correctly predicted 79.6 percent of the cases, that fails to be impressive. Had we predicted that all women who placed first would be nominated, and that none of the women who placed second in the initial primary would be nominated, we would have done almost as well (77.8 percent correct predictors). A few individual cases are predicted differently in the logit model, as opposed to the more simplified model set forth in the previous sentence.

In sum, the most important factor we have identified for determining the outcome of male-female runoffs is the order of finish for candidates in the first primary. Candidates who finish first in the initial primary have a strong chance of winning nomination in the runoff—regardless of gender. Once order of finish in the first primary is considered, the party or time at which the election occurs has little impact. Women running for the state legislature are somewhat more likely to be nominated but no more likely to receive a larger share of the runoff vote.

The Runoff as a Sexist Impediment

When women compete in a runoff, plurality leaders go on to win nomination at a particularly high rate. In female-male runoffs, the probability that the order of finish in the primary will be reversed in the second balloting is lower

Table 2.19 Multivariate Models of the Success of Women in Runoffs
(Standard Errors in Parentheses)

	Dependent Variables	
Variable	% of Vote	Winning Nomination
Intercept	.622	2.412
Woman's primary finish	−.091	−2.658
	(.011)	(.404)
Primary margin	−.121	.572
	(.080)	(.395)
Party	.001	−.461
	(.014)	(.500)
State legislative contest	.016	1.063
	(.015)	(.541)
1980s	.011	.466
	(.011)	(.391)
R^2	.314	
Adjusted R^2	.293	

Model chi square = 62.57

Correctly predicted = 79.6%

than in all-male contests. Front-running women have better odds of being
nominated than do men who led the primary and face another male in the
runoff. Contrary to the conventional wisdom, no evidence exists beyond the
episodic and anecdotal that runoffs discriminate against women who poll pluralities in the initial primary. Women who finish second in the opening primary, however, face stiff odds in the second election.

By dividing our data set into elections from the 1970s and those from
the 1980s, we show that women front-runners are doing better today than
in the past. If we were to marshal runoff data for earlier decades, it would
not be surprising to find lower success rates for women who led primaries.
The female-loses myth may have been accurate at some time prior to 1970,

but to the extent that it describes reality today, it applies only to statewide positions.

The infrequent successes enjoyed by women in runoffs for statewide offices is troublesome, but it must be recalled that primary leaders of both sexes generally do less well when seeking top-of-the-ticket positions. However, even accounting for the lower success rates for males statewide than for lower offices, women do worse statewide. The inability of women to overcome second-place finishes, except in state house contests, may be a remnant of antifeminist attitudes that contributes to the generally misleading notion that women usually lose runoffs.

The Fourth Myth: Race and the Runoff

At the heart of the debate over the runoff, as forcefully expressed by Jesse Jackson in the 1984 presidential campaign, lies the view that dual primaries stand as a major barrier to the electoral success of black candidates. Jackson and others have highlighted a few conspicuous cases to illustrate the inequities that seem to accompany a second primary. In light of the extensive public concern over this charge, and the related accusation that the dual primary serves as a disadvantage to women as well, we devote considerable attention to this aspect of the runoff debate.

The Jackson Critique

The most widely cited instance of alleged discrimination occurred in the Second District of North Carolina. On June 27, 1982, H. M. ("Mickey") Michaux, Jr., a black candidate for Congress who had previously served as a state legislator and a U.S. attorney, led the first primary with 44.5 percent of the vote. Trailing him were two white candidates: Tim Valentine, with 32.7 percent of the vote, and James Ramsey, with 22.8 percent. Had the contest ended there, Michaux would have been the Democratic nominee and might have gone on to be elected the first black U.S. representative from North Carolina since 1898, when Republican George White achieved that distinction. In the runoff primary, however, Valentine defeated Michaux by a margin of 53.6 percent, making Michaux, in the words of Harold W. Stanley, "the most prominent victim of what some consider the runoff's racial bias." In another case, Rev. Henry Ward, Jr., a black, sought the 1983 Democratic nomination for a seat in the Mississippi legislature. Several whites were also candidates, including the incumbent. Ward led the first primary but was eliminated in the second.[57]

Such outcomes have disillusioned some black politicians. "We must end the second primary before it ends us," declared Rev. Jackson in the 1984 presidential campaign, noting that "the runoff has devastated the impact of the Voting Rights Act [passed in 1965]."[58] For Jackson and other critics, the dual-primary arrangement was deeply rooted in America's history of racial discrimination and had to be weeded out of the electoral system.

In 1984 Jackson implied that he would seek to block black voter support for any White House aspirant who failed to acknowledge the need to eliminate the second-primary rule. In the spring of 1984, he seemed determined to force upon the platform committee of the approaching Democratic National Nominating Convention a "Jackson rule" calling on states to end the runoff procedure. Jackson's attempt to apply leverage—based on his influence over black voters—against the nominating convention and his fellow Democratic presidential aspirants was chiefly symbolic, as changes in individual state laws, rather than a Democratic platform statement, would be required to abolish the dual-primary system. Regardless, the issue had become for a time his litmus test for whether blacks ought to continue supporting the Democratic party. (Eventually, he backed the Democratic nominee for president, Walter Mondale, even though Mondale never urged abolition of the runoff.)

The vision driving Jackson and other blacks who advocated elimination of the runoff was one of increased electoral victories for candidates of their race. If a black candidate faced several white candidates in a single primary, the black might win nomination—even if only by a razor-thin plurality. A win would be a win, no matter how close. This is precisely what black mayoral candidate, Harold Washington, had accomplished in 1983 in Chicago, a city without a runoff provision for mayor. If forced into a runoff, however, a black candidate might face the combined forces of all the white candidates who had lost in the first primary—a sure formula for defeat in many constituencies without a black voting majority.

"Unintended Consequences" of the Jackson Rule

Critics of the Jackson rule—several of whom were sympathetic to the vision of black electoral successes held by Jesse Jackson—suggested that his cure might be worse than the disease. As Theodore H. White put it, the Jackson rule could well provide "a classic demonstration of the law of unintended consequences." [59] Even if blacks were to win more nominations in the absence of a runoff primary, what, critics asked, would these nominees face in the general election? There would be some victories to be sure, they said, but a great many more defeats as large numbers of white Democratic voters fled to the Republican party and its white nominee.

Nothing would so assist the rise of the GOP in the South, White and others have suggested, as a sudden upward surge in the number of blacks nominated by a minority of the Democratic party. With the ensuing sea change of party identification, Republican candidates (almost always white) would be able to defeat the Democratic black candidates in the general election. The end result would be more Republicans in office and, ironically, legislatures less sympathetic to the issues close to the hearts of black Americans.

"Nominations in one-round, wide-open Southern primaries might send dozens of black Congressmen to Washington by thin pluralities," noted White. "But it would also give enormous opportunities to Republicans to put down strong regional grassroots wherever whites fear blacks and seek alternatives." Or, as Bert Lance, then state chairman of Georgia's Democratic party, succinctly observed in 1984: "Quite simply, all [the Jackson rule] would do is help elect Republicans at every level." [60]

Other leading southern officeholders seem to agree. "[Abolition of the runoff] would build the Republican party overnight," stated U.S. Representative (now Senator) Wyche Fowler (D-Ga). "I think we'd probably elect somewhere between fifteen and twenty-five Republicans and only a couple or three blacks," added Fowler's House colleague Ed Jenkins (D-Ga). The Democratic party chairman in South Carolina, Bill Youngblood, regarded the Jackson rule as tantamount to handing the GOP "on a silver platter something we don't have now in our state—a grassroots organization." And Georgia's Lieutenant Governor (now Governor) Zell Miller predicted the polarization of his state "along racial lines" if the runoff were prohibited.[61]

The Runoff: A Boon for Blacks?

Other observers wary of a rush to the Jackson rule argued that preservation of the runoff might actually benefit some black candidates and others with a history of disadvantage in American electoral politics. As former Georgia state legislator Julian Bond has written, "[The runoff] actually discriminates against the numerical minority, black *or white*, in elections in which there is racial polarization."[62] Andrew Young, the black civil rights leader and former mayor of Atlanta, had experiential grounds for his comparable skepticism about Jackson's charge that the runoff was discriminatory: he had placed second in the initial mayoral primary of 1981 but went on to a runoff victory.

Some experts have suggested that runoffs can actually improve the electoral prospects of black candidates in districts with black majorities. Without the runoff, notes Harold Stanley, black candidates might "split the black vote and allow a white candidate to gain a plurality nomination." Stanley quotes the chairman of the Black Caucus in South Carolina's state house: " 'Things have changed [since reapportionment and the advent of several districts with black majorities] so that the runoffs now can work in our favor.' "[63]

Advantages from the runoff accruing to black candidates have become even more pronounced following the redistricting of the early 1990s. The modification of the Voting Rights Act in 1982 rewrote the rules for drawing minority districts. To successfully challenge a districting plan, minorities need only show that the proposal dilutes their political influence. During the last round of redistricting in 1981–82, claims of racial discrimination had to prove that there had been an intent to discriminate in order to succeed. Now all that minorities must show is that a reapportionment plan has the effect of diluting their influence. It appears, then, that minority districts must be created whenever possible—an interpretation adopted by the Justice Department when reviewing the plans of political units that must have their legislation affecting elections preapproved before being implemented.

Pressure to maximize the number of districts in which minorities constitute a majority of the population has expanded the situations in which, following the Jackson logic, a runoff should help, not hurt, black candidates. One possibility is that majority-black districts will be made less heavily black. For example, three districts each of which was 75 percent black might be replaced by four districts each having black populations of 56 to 57 percent. Another possibility is that black populations from several districts in which blacks constituted a minority might be combined to form a district with a narrow black majority. Of course, by extracting minority populations from some districts to create new minority-majority districts, the remaining districts become more heavily white.

What does redistricting have to do with the majority-vote requirement? The answer is potentially a lot! Districts with black majorities, especially newly created black majority districts, are more likely to attract multiple black candidates and a single white rather than the multiple whites and single black candidate that Jesse Jackson envisioned. A white incumbent who resides in a district that has recently been given a black majority may face more than one black challenger in the first postredistricting election. The advantages of a white incumbent are magnified if, in order to bring together a black majority, curiously shaped districts are drawn that meander across extensive portions of a state, as has been proposed in several runoff states. A white incumbent with greater name recognition and easier access to campaign funds from political action committees will be the odds-on favorite to poll a plurality if challenged by multiple blacks.

As Julian Bond noted in the quotation presented earlier, a black majority in the district will not guarantee the nomination of a black if the campaign field contains multiple blacks opposing a single white. The likelihood of a black being nominated in a majority-black district is enhanced if the first primary reduces the number of black candidates, allowing the survivor to try and overtake a single white in the runoff. Of course, if a black led the field in the initial primary, then assuming that the primary leader can retain the loyalty of black voters in a majority-black district, the black will defeat the white in the runoff. To summarize: the scenario that Jesse Jackson saw as allowing whites to rally behind a single white in order to defeat a black who led in the primary could have just the opposite effect in a majority-black district.

The reapportionment of the 1990s reduced the number of districts in which the Jackson scenario is likely. If we accept Jackson's assumption that a black candidate cannot attract enough white votes to win a majority, then for a black to place first against multiple whites yet fail to obtain a majority, blacks must be a sizable share of population but less than a majority. The creation of additional majority-black districts means that there are fewer districts where blacks constitute a sizable minority. For example, in a plan adopted by the Georgia General Assembly in 1991 for its lower chamber, 54 percent of the state's black population would reside in a majority-black district. A third of all black Georgians would live in districts where blacks constituted less than 30 percent of the population—a situation in which it is improbable that a black would lead a primary field on the strength of black votes alone. If a black population of 30 to 50 percent is necessary to create the conditions for the Jackson scenario, only one in eight Georgia blacks would be potentially affected.

The Georgia plan outlined above was rejected by the Justice Department, meaning that an even larger share of the black population will have to be placed in majority-black districts before a plan can be implemented. Consequently, far more blacks will live in districts where a runoff may be helpful rather than harmful—even if Jesse Jackson's basic assumption is correct.

Some observers have pointed out that the absence of a runoff could play into the hands of bigoted white candidates pandering to racists (the segregationists or "seg-forever" vote).[64] In 1974, for example, segregationist Lester Maddox floated to the top to win the first primary in Georgia's Democratic gubernatorial nomination with 36 percent of the vote. Under a single-primary system, he might have been nominated. Instead, Maddox had to face the runner-up, George Busbee, in a second primary. Moderate voters, who proved to be in a majority, gave Busbee a victory in the runoff. He easily defeated his Republican opponent in the general election. In this instance, the runoff served as a barrier to an antiblack candidate.

The defeat of race-baiter Orval Faubus of Arkansas in a 1970 gubernatorial runoff offers another classic illustration. In Mississippi and South Carolina, recent progressive candidates favored by black voters—Governors William Winter and Richard Riley, respectively—also won Democratic nominations thanks to the runoff provision. Under a single-primary rule, both men would have been defeated.[65]

At the same time, it should be noted that in some runoffs the more conservative candidate has won, as in the case of Maddox's earlier bid for the governorship in 1966. In his study of gubernatorial candidates' racial stands, Earl Black found that the advantage accorded segregationist candidates in runoffs had largely passed by the mid-1960s. Thereafter, the black vote was a sufficiently large component of the Democratic primary that racist appeals were counterproductive.[66]

The "Seg" Vote

The bottom line, most opponents of the Jackson rule have concluded, is that, in the words of columnist Tom Wicker, "black-white voting is likely to be an unfortunate fact of life—not only in the South—for some time to come, whether or not runoffs are abolished."[67] In 1982 Representative Robert C. Clark, the first black to serve in the Mississippi state legislature in the twentieth century, won the Democratic party's congressional nomination in the first primary with a clear majority over several white candidates and thereby avoided a runoff. At that point he received the endorsement of the state's leading Democratic officeholders, including the governor, William Winter. In the general election, however, a white Republican candidate narrowly defeated Clark by a 50.3 percent margin.

Julian Bond has stated the appropriate conclusion to be drawn from the Clark race: "Winning the primary doesn't always guarantee winning general elections, even in nominally Democratic Mississippi." Bond acknowledges that although "eliminating the majority vote requirement will make it easier for blacks to win some primaries, . . . it won't make winning general elections—the ones that count—easier." The sweet taste of victory in the runoff can quickly turn to ashes in a general election defeat. Andrew Young concludes similarly that black politicians lose not because of the runoff rule, but because of racism in the white electorate. Racism is unlikely to disappear overnight by nailing new planks into the Democratic party platform, as Rev. Jackson would have it. "Since the runoff is not the cause of the electoral defeats of black candidates," maintains Harold Stanley, "ending the runoff will not provide the cure." [68]

At present, argue opponents of the Jackson rule, the hard reality for black candidates seems to be that, absent a black majority in the constituency, their electoral fortunes are dim under any electoral rules. Conservative voters— and, at the extreme, the segregationist or "seg" vote—remain the chief obstacle to the election of blacks, not the runoff primary.

Regardless, the Jackson camp sometimes has retorted that if the number of blacks nominated by a plurality increases—with a few more blacks than usual actually going on to win the general election—then this result alone would make abolition of the runoff a worthwhile objective. "Black candidates have to win the nomination before they can have a chance of winning an election," points out Thomas Cavanagh, formerly a political analyst at the Joint Center for Policy Studies in Washington, D.C. Prohibition of the runoff would be worthwhile, some say, even if large numbers of seg-forever voters defected permanently from the Democratic party. "So what if 400,000 or 500,000 whites defect?" asked Mickey Michaux after his runoff defeat in North Carolina. [69]

Harold Stanley offers a response: only once in North Carolina since 1948 have the Democrats won a U.S. Senate or gubernatorial contest by more than 500,000 votes (the exception was the 1976 governor's race, which was won by 517,191 votes). Michaux's mathematics fails to sum, writes Stanley, to "a winning strategy" for Tarheel Democrats. [70]

Shadowy Origins of the Runoff

The contention that the original purpose of the dual primary was racially motivated has been called into question. According to Julian Bond, the runoff was "introduced at the turn of the century in order to block Populists from gaining public office," at a time when most blacks were already barred from the ballot box by a range of imaginative legal restrictions—from poll taxes to literacy tests. Stanley concurs. "The runoff cannot be viewed as an important component of the southern attempt to squelch black political influence," he writes, "because of the potent limits on black participation in place before the adoptions of the runoff." [71]

However, others, such as Peyton McCrary, reasoned that "southern politicians were . . . aware that many of those disenfranchising provisions wouldn't last long. The runoff served as a second line of defense against the possibility of a black being elected to any significant office." [72] But McCrary seems to be using that twenty-twenty hindsight that improves the coaching of all Monday-morning quarterbacks. None of the major discussions of the disfranchisement and dilution of black voters in the South point to the runoff as an obstacle. Nor is there evidence that as disfranchising techniques such as the white primary, literacy test, and poll tax fell, southern politicians consoled themselves or their racist constituents by pointing to the majority-vote requirement as a bulwark against black political influence. [73]

Our data do not address this historical aspect of the runoff debate. In chapters 3 and 4, however, we review the findings reached in contemporary legal cases involving black and white candidates in runoff primaries, and we present our own analyses of biracial contests in a variety of dual-primary settings in recent decades. Accordingly, we now shift to a descriptive and legalistic examination of two runoff cases involving charges of racial bias, one in New York City and the other in Arkansas.

3 Legal Challenges to the Runoff

"It is a miracle that New York works at all," concluded E. B. White in his celebrated essay on America's largest city. "The whole thing is implausible." [1] As implausible as New York City may have seemed to White in 1949, with its—even then—bewildering maze of subterranean sewer and steam pipes, gas mains, telephone and power lines, its angry swarm of yellow taxicabs, dazed tourists, and maniacal bus drivers, its steel and concrete canyons with rushing rivers of brusque professionals, hucksters, and the dispossessed, today the "Big Apple" has become an even more complex microcosm of American society. It approaches traffic gridlock twice each day as those who work in the city head across the bridges and through the tunnels (the "B and T crowd") that connect Manhattan to the surrounding suburbs where they live. It has more practicing psychiatrists than any metropolis in the world; its ethnic tensions are palpable, its politics byzantine. Yet, miraculously, the city continues to function.

The city's political strains have become as self-evident as the human and automobile congestion. They surfaced clearly during the 1988 New York presidential primary. Mayor Edward Koch further aggravated tensions between black and Jewish citizens with his acid criticisms of black Democratic candidate Jesse Jackson. "Jews would have to be crazy to vote for Jackson," Koch opined, with apparent reference to the candidate's ties with pro-Arab groups in the United States and abroad and Jackson's private reference in 1984 to Jews as "Hymies"—a term of derision for which Jackson had duly apologized.

The New York Runoff Debate

The Koch-Jackson quarrel was symptomatic of the ever-simmering racial un-
rest that continues to plague New York City, just as it does much of the nation.
In 1984 this unrest took the form of a protracted and often heated legal battle
over whether the runoff primary procedure had been adopted for the city of
New York by the state's white-dominated legislature to discourage black and
Hispanic electoral opportunities for achieving citywide office.

The Badillo-Wagner Mayoral Race of 1969

The peculiar outcome of the 1969 mayoral race in New York City prompted
the state legislature to adopt a runoff procedure for selected political offices
in the city. Victory in the Democratic primary that year went to Mario
Proccacino, whose views on the issues—he ran as a conservative, "safe
streets" candidate—fell outside the mainstream of the party regulars. Proccacino's unexpected nomination, with only 33 percent of the popular vote,
resulted from a split in the support of party regulars between Herman Badillo
and Robert Wagner, who received 28 percent and 29 percent of the popular
vote, respectively. Only 30 percent of the registered Democrats had bothered
to vote, and two-thirds of them supported the moderate to liberal candidates.
When Proccacino walked away with the nomination, Democratic regulars—
repelled by his right-wing views—sat out the general election. As a consequence, Proccacino lost to incumbent John V. Lindsay, who himself had lost
the Republican primary earlier and was forced to stand as the candidate of the
minor Independent and Liberal parties. The freak nomination in the Democratic primary of a fringe candidate, who had achieved victory in a badly
divided contest, and the subsequent reelection of Lindsay were bitter pills for
Democratic regulars to swallow.

    After this experience—which *New York Times* editorialists called an "ab-
surdity"—several Democratic officials in the city sponsored a runoff bill in
the state legislature to avoid the future nomination of splinter candidates like
Proccacino.[2] Their bill would require a successful candidate to receive 40 percent of the popular vote to gain nomination in the initial primary or else face

a runoff. If Democrats were going to win elections, concluded these officials, their nominees would have to exhibit broad-based support among the sundry groups that made up the party.

Although, on the surface, this argument seemed to make sense and had widespread appeal among party regulars, some black and Hispanic leaders sounded an early warning that the runoff procedure—whatever the true intent of its sponsors—might bar minority candidates from citywide office. The recommended 40 percent threshold was just above the percentage of the combined black-Hispanic population in New York City at the time. (It was problematic, at best, that blacks and Hispanics would vote together, especially for a black candidate.)[3] Yet, proponents of the 40 percent standard pointed out, anything less than this mark might again produce another Proccacino—that is, a nominee with insufficient support among the party's constituents.

Some minority city politicians further suggested that what really disturbed white Democrats in 1969 was less Proccacino's upset nomination than the surprisingly high percentage of votes tallied by Herman Badillo, who was of Puerto Rican descent and the first Hispanic candidate to contest the Democratic nomination for mayor of New York City. In their view, the "Badillo scare" represented the hidden agenda of "reformers." In fact, in Albany's legislative circles the runoff proposal was often referred to as the "anti-Badillo bill." A black Democratic state senator from the Bronx, Joseph L. Galiber, warned that with the proposed runoff law, "under the guise of liberalism, under the guise of democracy, a minority [political candidate] could not win in the next fifty or sixty years in the City of New York, notwithstanding the fact that it represents a large portion." Galiber concluded, ominously, that "if the Republican Party ever wanted to singly destroy the Democratic Party, this is the bill."[4]

Despite criticism from some quarters in the minority community—as well as from (among other more establishment figures) Mayor Lindsay, who complained that the runoff procedure, though perhaps sound in theory, would incur for the city of New York "a substantial and unnecessary expenditure"—the runoff bill introduced in 1972 by Democratic state assemblymen Stanley Steingut and Albert Blumenthal raced through both legislative chambers without debate.[5] The state senate approved the bill by a vote of 49–8 and the assembly by a vote of 104–5.[6] Notwithstanding Galiber's warning, every minority member of the assembly and the senate present and voting supported the bill: five out of eleven assemblymen and one out of four senators. In little over a month, Governor Nelson Rockefeller signed the bill into law. The statute provided that if any candidate for the offices of mayor, city council president, or comptroller of the city of New York failed to receive 40 percent of the popular vote cast in a party's general primary, then the board of elections would conduct a runoff between the top two vote getters.

The purpose of the law, stated Steingut and Blumenthal, was to prevent another Proccacino "fluke." They sought to encourage coalition building instead of nomination outcomes determined by single-issue voting.[7] While a few minority legislators demurred, a leading Hispanic member of the state senate, Robert Garcia, spoke in favor of the measure and claimed that Herman Badillo himself, at the time a congressman, supported it. (Years later, when the battle over the runoff moved into the courts, Badillo testified that he could not recall having endorsed the Steingut-Blumenthal bill—though he did not deny the possibility.)[8] Although the arguments pro and con continued to brew, one outcome was indisputable: the New York City runoff provision had passed into law with relative ease. Events would soon prove, however, that it faced a stormy future.

Challenges from the Right and the Left

The first challenge to the new runoff provision came not from the minority community but from Mario Proccacino, the beneficiary in 1969 of the vicissitudes of fractured voting. His suit argued that the state legislature had no right to determine the electoral methods used by the city of New York and, further, that the runoff provision violated his due process rights as a voter. The Supreme Court of New York County rejected both arguments on the grounds that, first, the legislature had acted properly on a subject that was of concern statewide and, second, rather than violating due process, the runoff method established "a more valid consensus of the party members."[9]

As the runoff law was applied to specific electoral contests, its critics within some groups in New York City began to grow. The second-primary provision was triggered in three elections: the 1973 and 1977 mayoral races and the 1977 city council presidential race. In 1973 four candidates entered the initial Democratic primary election for mayor: Abraham Beame, the irrepressible Herman Badillo, Congressman Mario Biaggi, and Albert Blumenthal, one of the original cosponsors of the runoff proposal in the state assembly. At the end of the initial balloting, the results were as follows: Beame 34.5 percent; Badillo, 29.0 percent; Biaggi, 20.5 percent; and Blumenthal, 16.0 percent. In the runoff, Beame won with 61 percent, compared to Badillo's 39 percent.

In 1977 the mayoral field swelled to seven candidates, including incumbent Beame; Bella Abzug, an outspoken feminist and member of the U.S. House of Representatives; Edward Koch, a former member of the House; Mario Cuomo, who would later become governor of New York; Percy Sutton, Manhattan Borough president and the first black person to seek the Democratic party nomination; and, again, Herman Badillo, who was rapidly becoming the Harold Stassen of New York City's mayoralty elections. The initial balloting produced these results: Edward Koch, 20.0 percent; Mario Cuomo, 19.0 percent; Abraham Beame, 18.0 percent; Bella Abzug, 16.5 percent; Percy Sutton, 14.0 percent; Herman Badillo, 11.0 percent; and Joel Harnett, 1.5 percent. In the runoff, Koch retained his first-place standing with 55 percent of the vote. As in 1973, either a plurality or a runoff procedure would have produced the same outcome; in this contest, Koch won. Yet critics of the second primary became preoccupied with a runoff landscape in New York City that seemed, to them, to be littered with the bodies of defeated minorities and now, with Abzug's loss, a noted feminist as well.

The 1977 contest for city council president, though, would shatter the pattern of white male dominance under the runoff rule. The initial results in this primary were Paul O'Dwyer, 31 percent; Carol Bellamy, 25 percent; Carter Burden, 20 percent; Abraham Hirschfeld, 17 percent; and Leonard Stavisky, 7 percent. Incumbent O'Dwyer then took a thumping from Bellamy, who managed to garner 59 percent of the vote in the second primary and then went on to win the general election.

Neither the 1977 victory of a female underdog nor the fact that Herman Badillo—the only black or Hispanic person to make it to the runoff stage in New York City—had been given two chances at winning the nomination because of the runoff opportunity in 1973 failed to quell growing dissatisfaction among minorities with the second-primary law. Not even the basic arithmetic that an Abzug-Sutton-Badillo coalition in 1977 could have tallied 41.5 percent of the vote in the first primary—if these three reformers had rallied behind just one candidate among themselves—seemed to carry much weight.[10] The left wing of the Democratic party soon took its case to the courts.

Rejection of the Runoff Rule

In October 1984, Rev. Calvin O. Butts III, a black, and Digna Sanchez, a Hispanic, filed a class action suit against the runoff. From June 3 to June 10, 1985, Judge Charles L. Brieant, Jr., heard the case in a bench (nonjury) trial before the Federal District Court for the Southern District of New York.

The heart of the case against the runoff advanced by Butts and Sanchez rested on Section 2 of the Voting Rights Act, as amended in 1982. As stipulated by this amendment, successful challenges to existing electoral arrangements could be made by minorities if they demonstrated that the status quo had the effect of diluting their political strength. No longer was it necessary to demonstrate that the dilutive effect had been intended; thus, it was now easier for plaintiffs to win legal challenges to election procedures. Under Section 2, plaintiffs prevail if, "based on the Totality of Circumstances, it is shown that the processes leading to the nomination or election in the state or political subdivision are not equally open to participation by members of a political class of citizens protected by [this legislation] in that its members have less opportunity than other members of the electorate to participate in the political process and to elect representatives of their choice."

Congress set out seven major and two minor conditions for the courts to consider in applying the so-called Totality of Circumstances test. Among these conditions are the degree of racial polarization in voting, the number of minority group members who have been elected, and a catchall set of *enhancement factors*. Enhancement factors consist of those electoral variables—including the majority-vote requirement—that allegedly increase the likelihood of minority-vote dilution. For the plaintiffs to succeed in the New York case, they would have to demonstrate that the runoff provision diluted their political opportunities. Constitutional claims are normally asserted in law suits on voting rights; however, because it is necessary to demonstrate an intent to discriminate in order to prevail on the constitutional claim, courts rarely decide cases on this basis.

Plaintiffs Butts and Sanchez argued that the runoff provision robbed voters in the city's black and Hispanic communities of their rights to equal protection and due process. In their view, the runoff had been designed, all too success-fully, to throw up a barrier between minorities and the possibility of winning the three major citywide offices. As members of the Metropolitan Black Bar Association would argue in an amicus curiae brief, "The so-called runoff primary rule has effectively furthered the rule of the majority populace within the City of New York to the continued exclusion of Blacks and Hispanics." [11]

In a companion brief, the National Association for the Advancement of Colored People (NAACP) declared that the runoff statute had been "moti-vated by discriminatory animus"—legal jargon for racism. [12] In contrast, the defendants—the city of New York and its board of elections—maintained that the statute had never been meant to have a discriminatory effect against any social, racial, or ethnic group in the city and, in fact, had never had such an effect. The battle lines were drawn for a major legal test of the runoff rule.

Time and Money

Whatever his views may have been back when the runoff idea was wending its way through the Albany legislature in 1969, Herman Badillo by 1984 had become a vocal opponent of the procedure. In one of the most damaging indictments of the runoff, Badillo charged that it gave advantages to wealthier, established (read: white) candidates because of the importance of money and media advertising in the brief period between the first and second primaries (twenty-one days).

"There are two types of campaigns," Badillo testified before Judge Brie-ant. "One is a media campaign based on money. The other one is a street campaign based upon your physical presence in the neighborhoods." Lacking the large campaign war chest often enjoyed by white candidates, Badillo had developed the art of street campaigning to a fare-thee-well. Yet, he concluded, "the media campaign can be a short campaign, and that's what the runoff is geared for." [13]

When it came to fund-raising, Badillo knew few "fat cats" who would cough up $10,000–$15,000 with a quick signature on a check; rather, he had to rely on dinners and cocktail parties. "It takes time to set up a dinner, because you have to send a mailing out and get on the phone and call up people," he lamented. "If you are dependent on dinners and cocktail parties, by definition a short campaign of less than three weeks would make it very difficult to raise significant amounts of money." [14] Lawyers for the city of New York conceded that the runoff was increasingly an expensive media event, but they insisted that the importance of television spots and the need to raise large sums of money to buy them were problems associated with elections of various stripes throughout the United States "and are not unique to a runoff primary election." [15]

The brevity of the runoff period also encourages last-minute negative campaigning, claimed critics of the runoff provision. Certainly, anti-Badillo literature with racist overtones was distributed to voters during the second primary in 1973, giving him precious little time to refute charges that he favored quotas in hiring and education and was anti-Jewish. As Badillo recalled, "you have the kind of panic that you can set off on a one-to-one campaign where there is a limited period of time because you don't have enough time to overcome this, you don't have enough time to conduct an investigation." [16] Nevertheless, such negative techniques can be—and often are—used at the last minute in various types of political campaigns, not just runoffs.

Voting Blocs and Type of Office

Another leading minority politician in New York City, Percy Sutton, reinforced Badillo's criticism of the runoff provision in testimony before Judge Brieant. In Sutton's view, blacks and Hispanics during the sixties had moved a long way toward expanding their base of registered voters and consolidating their political base in the city (though, according to census surveys, minority registration continued to lag behind that of whites). Minorities had reached a position, Sutton argued, where they could command a sizable plurality in many city elections—yet not the 40 percent plurality mandated by the Steingut-Blumenthal bill. According to his testimony, "if a plurality was needed only, a possibility was there for winning a primary election and being the designee of the party." Moreover, Sutton continued, even if a minority candidate somehow made it into the second primary, he or she would be "pitted against one of those three or four, two or three other persons who were in the primary, and if people were to exercise their prejudices and it was to be exercised negatively, then [the minority candidate] would lose the [runoff] election." [17]

For some witnesses, the entire topic reduced to numbers and voting blocs. If the minority voting population in New York City were 50 percent or more, instead of some 33 percent at the time, the 40 percent rule and the runoff provision would have troubled blacks and Hispanics far less. As one expert witness concluded, in a constituency where racial bloc voting exists, the runoff statute benefits that faction enjoying a population of 50 percent or more. It was only a matter of time, and procreation, before the provisions present disadvantages for minorities could turn into advantages. "If we assume that the minority population of New York City is 50 percent or more in the near future," concluded the witness, it was "definitely possible that the runoff statute would benefit minority candidates." [18]

Former New York lieutenant governor Basil Paterson, a black politician who managed to attract an eye-opening 86 percent of the statewide vote in 1970 in a contested Democratic primary election for that position—winning sixty-one of the state's sixty-two counties—introduced another variable into the debate: the significance of the office being sought. He candidly attributed his remarkable electoral success as a minority candidate to a perception among white voters that the office of lieutenant governor was without "any consequence." [19] In New York City itself, blacks had similarly won selected offices by landslide margins. In 1965 Constance Baker Motley won the contested Democratic primary for Manhattan Borough president with 87 percent of the vote against a white candidate. In 1969, among other examples, Percy Sutton garnered 81 percent of the votes in the Democratic primary for the same office. Yet, suggested Paterson in his testimony, for more important offices, like the governorship or the mayorship of New York City, white voters became more circumspect and were reluctant to cast their ballots for minority candidates. This racially polarized voting, he maintained, loaded the dice against black and Hispanic politicians when a 40 percent rule was in effect.

Runoff Reversal

Paterson's argument strongly influenced Judge Brieant. "If white voters are reluctant to 'cross-over' and vote for a minority candidate for Mayor, as the 1973 runoff election returns suggest," the judge would conclude in his opinion, "then [the runoff law] enhances this tendency by increasing the effectiveness of negative racial campaign tactics during a short runoff campaign period." The question in Brieant's mind was twofold: Could a minority candidate expect to make it into the runoff phase with a "diabolic" 40 percent threshold, and, even if the answer were occasionally yes (as Badillo had proven), could he or she hope to win the runoff when costly media promotion seemed to be so vital to success? The judge was doubtful: "Historical evidence of past inequality when combined with evidence of lower socioeconomic status and lower rates of voter registration, supports a finding that a plaintiff class member has less opportunity to nominate and elect a candidate of choice under a statute which requires a superplurality in the initial primary election (40 percent), or the burdens associated with running two primary campaigns." [20]

Pronouncing the issues "clear," and expressing (without explaining) a preference for a 30 percent runoff threshold, Brieant decided in favor of the plaintiffs on August 13, 1985.[21] Within a fortnight, city officials initiated an appeals process in the U.S. Court of Appeals for the Second Circuit.

Act Two: The Appeals Process

At the request of attorneys representing New York City and the state of New York, the court of appeals expedited the appeals process, with the panel's three judges, Mssrs. Lumbard, Oakes, and Newman, listening to the arguments on September 17, 1985. In a preliminary brief for the appeals court, the attorney general of New York State, Robert Abrams, and his team of lawyers recapitulated the major points in favor of the runoff law. By now the themes were familiar to those who had followed the earlier skirmishes.

The State's Case

The purpose of the runoff procedure, the state maintained, was "to encourage coalition building, and avoidance of the dangers of single issue voting." The runoff was, therefore, more likely to "elect a candidate who is ideologically and politically accountable to a broad spectrum of the members of the party." Moreover, every minority legislator present at the time in Albany had voted for the Steingut-Blumenthal bill, and Herman Badillo and Percy Sutton themselves had reportedly supported the measure. Further, argued Abrams, the minority community could win citywide elections under this provision if only it would vote more cohesively: "To the extent a black and Hispanic coalition exists, it can garner 40 percent of the vote in a Democratic Party primary." Sutton had conceded during the bench trial in June that in a three-way contest with two minority office seekers, the runoff provision could help one of the minority candidates.[22] Cassius put it poetically: "The fault, dear Brutus, is not in our stars but in ourselves." For the state's top law enforcement officer, the fault lay not in the runoff provision but in the political quarrels that divided the minority community.

As for Badillo's charge that a runoff encouraged negative campaigning, because its constricted time period prohibited a response, Abrams pointed out that dirty campaign tactics "can be made at the last minute with the same intended effect in the longest of campaigns." On what seemed to be less firm footing, he also rejected the plaintiffs' allegation that official discrimination had plagued New York City's electoral processes, noting that recently party leaders often sought a "'balanced ticket' where different candidates for different offices possessing different local or racial or ethnic appeal would add to the strength of each other by running as a slate or team." The state concluded that Judge Brieant's "finding of such prior official discrimination is, therefore, not supported by the evidence and should be found to be clearly erroneous." This was the bottom line for the state attorney general: "The requirement that there be a runoff where no candidate for citywide office obtains 40 percent of the vote in the primary is simply not what is responsible for minorities' inability to date to win the highest elected offices in New York City."[23]

The City Weighs In

New York City's attorneys, led by Frederick A. O. Schwarz, Jr., the corporation counsel of the city of New York and grandson of the famous toy manufacturer, joined the argument against Judge Brieant's decision. Sounding like a panel of political scientists, the lawyers presented a complex, multivariate portrait of city elections, based on a set of conditions that made the future effect of the runoff provision, in their view, "entirely speculative." These conditions included "the degree of voter participation within the white and minority communities, the number of white and minority candidates, the ideological position and strength of the various candidates, the extent to which black and Hispanic voters vote together, and the issues that are of primary concern to the electorate."[24]

Moreover, they emphasized, the electoral victories of Mayor Beame and Mayor Koch demonstrated that a clear-cut majority choice could emerge under the runoff rule. Carol Bellamy's success showed that even a powerful incumbent could be upset in a runoff. The city also expressed bewilderment over Brieant's unelaborated notion that, somehow, the 10 percent difference between a 40 and a 30 percent threshold was pivotal to the integrity of a runoff. Above all, Brieant had "ignored the most relevant (and undisputed) evidence, *i.e.*, that in the thirteen-year history of the statute, not one minority candidate has been denied a party nomination because of the runoff." Herman Badillo, the only minority candidate to participate in a runoff in New York City, "would not have been the Democratic Party nominee [in 1973] if the 40% rule did not apply," added the attorneys. "Mr. Badillo was in fact benefited [by the second-primary provision], in that he was provided with the opportunity to build a successful coalition in the run-off. His failure to do so can in no way be attributed to the run-off statute."[25]

The city's bottom line was this: "This run-off statute is a racially neutral

law, designed for a proper democratic purpose, which has operated to implement that purpose without any racially discriminatory effect."[26] Because the
existing law was discriminatory in neither purpose nor effect, the judgment
of the district court should be reversed.

The Runoff Is Reinstated

By a vote of two to one (with Judge Oakes dissenting), the appeals court
reversed Charles Brieant's judgment and dismissed the plaintiffs' complaint.
The two prorunoff judges seemed to be swayed, according to the opinion
written by Judge C. J. Lumbard, by the defendants' arguments that the
Steingut-Blumenthal bill had been overwhelmingly embraced by state legislators (including the black and Hispanic members present) in order to avoid
future Proccacino-like splinter candidates, not because of discriminatory intent. "The 40% threshold . . . was obviously chosen because Proccacino
received 33% of the vote in 1969," wrote Lumbard, "not because of the
minority population figures in New York."[27] Recalling the case of Carol Bellamy's runoff victory over "insider" Paul O'Dwyer in the 1977 campaign for
city council president and Herman Badillo's second chance to win the mayoralty nomination in 1973, the opinion emphasized that the second-primary
rule actually "may *help* a minority candidate to win nomination." The runoff
was back in business.

In his dissent, Judge Oakes expressed concern that "no minority candidate has been elected to any of the three offices so affected [by the runoff
rule]." He remained convinced that, under the requirement of a 40 percent
superplurality, members of the plaintiffs' class had "less opportunity to
nominate and elect a candidate of choice."[28] The brevity of time, expense
(an estimated extra half-million dollars), and "dynamics" of a closed primary that seemed to encourage racial polarization all worked, Oakes opined,
to the disadvantage of minority candidates. Particularly troubling to him
was the short time allocated to the runoff campaign (three weeks). This, he
believed, allowed the opponents of minority candidates the potential opportunity to use racial appeals that could never be answered adequately before
the runoff.

Two further points nagged at Oakes. First, he was disturbed that New York City was the only metropolis to have a runoff primary among the seventeen major cities in the United States "with minority populations large enough to support a black or Hispanic mayoral candidacy, but not so large as fully to dominate the political scene." (The judge failed to comment on Badillo's advance to the second primary in 1973.) Second, Oakes declared, in an essentially one-party town like New York City, a closed primary preceding a runoff allowed a cohesive white majority to keep a minority candidate off the ballot for the general election. If, instead, the Democratic primary were open, Oakes concluded opaquely, elections would involve no more discrimination "than is inherent in the size of the voting group." As to whether the 30 percent threshold advocated by Brieant would correct the alleged discriminatory tilt of the Steingut-Blumenthal 40 percent benchmark, Oakes stated simply that he "did not reach that question." [29]

The Score in New York City:
Plaintiffs Two, Defendants Two

The Lumbard and Newman votes summed to a majority at the critical juncture—the court of appeals—and as a result victory lay with the defendants. The official pronouncement of the judges—"The judgment is reversed with direction to dismiss the complaint"—rang down from the bench with a resounding finality, insomuch as anything is ever "final" in the shifting sands of American jurisprudence.

The accuracy of the conclusion reached by the majority on the court of appeals was demonstrated in 1989, when David Dinkins, a black, won the Democratic nomination for mayor with 51 percent of the vote and went on to victory in the general election. Dinkins achieved his success not in an open-seat contest, but by defeating three-term incumbent Ed Koch. An exit poll conducted by the *New York Times* and CBS News showed that Dinkins polled 30 percent of the white vote along with 94 percent of the black vote. Obviously, achieving 40 percent of the vote was possible for a black mayoral candidate in New York City—the arguments of the *Butts* plaintiffs notwithstanding.

The Courts and the Runoff in the South

The initial judicial challenge to the runoff in the South came from Mississippi. While rumors floated around that state that the U.S. Department of Justice had compiled a list of one hundred runoffs in which the black candidate had failed to win nomination, the plaintiffs dropped this suit before it came to trial. Consequently, the first southern challenge to be fully adjudicated came from Arkansas. As with *Butts*, the Arkansas suit was decided under Section 2 of the Voting Rights Act, although the plaintiffs offered some evidence of an intent to discriminate in the dual-primary system.

In May 1988, following a bench trial, Judge Garnett Thomas Eisele of the U.S. District Court, Eastern District of Arkansas, dismissed a challenge to the majority-rule voting requirement in Arkansas. The case, *Whitfield v. Democratic Party of the State of Arkansas*, contested the state's dual-primary provision, which had been established in 1938 after several years of controversy involving the electoral victories of various splinter candidates.[30] In 1932, for example, the ballot for the Democratic primary in some counties was as large as a tablecloth. Seven candidates stood for the gubernatorial nomination and seven more for the U.S. Senate nomination; six ran for the office of lieutenant governor. When the dust settled on primary day in this one-party state, a number of winners had failed to obtain a majority of the votes cast. The nominee for governor, J. M. Futrell, polled less than 45 percent of the vote (in 1928, the Democratic nominee for governor had tallied less than 42 percent), and the nominee for lieutenant governor, Lee Cazort, garnered less than 31 percent.

Origins of the Arkansas Runoff

Arkansas Democratic activists vowed to do something about this situation, which they viewed as antimajoritarian and, therefore, undemocratic. In Little Rock, a group of influential citizens formed the Run-Off Primary Association, a lobbying group to advocate the adoption of a second-primary provision. Governor Futrell quickly embraced the movement, declaring in his inaugural address of January 1933 that "by no means should an insubstantial minority be allowed to make a nomination." The runoff law raced through the Arkansas legislature, with a senate vote of 28 to 0 in January 1933 and a house vote of 84 to 3 the next month. Without delay, Futrell signed into law Act 38 of 1933.

Act 38 had a short life. During elections in 1933 and 1934, the runoff procedure drew sharp criticism in some parts of the state. The first electoral contest to be held following the passage of Act 38 was a special election in 1933 to fill the vacated seat of Congressman Heartstill Ragon, a Democrat. Brooks Hays polled a plurality during the opening vote of the Democratic primary. He lost the runoff to D. D. Terry, however, apparently in large measure because the third, eliminated candidate, Sam Rorex, threw his support behind Terry. For some, this outcome discredited the new procedure.

In 1934 the runoff method produced another "victim," J. Oscar Humphrey, the incumbent state auditor. Although in the initial balloting Humphrey outpolled his closest competitor by 41,463 votes, in the runoff he came up short by a margin of 100,204 to 95,516 votes behind Charles Parker. Critics looked upon both of these widely reported results as "examples of political 'tampering' and 'trading.'"[31] Questions were raised as well about the added cost to Arkansas taxpayers of holding a second primary.

Bowing in part to these criticisms, the state legislature repealed the runoff statute in 1935. (Key politicians from "machine" counties evidently also preferred the larger opportunities for their own control over nominations offered by plurality rather than majority electoral procedures.) Incensed by this setback, runoff proponents took up the crusade for a political remedy that would avoid the volatility of legislative coalitions: a runoff amendment firmly lodged in the Arkansas Constitution, safe from easy reversals in the state house and senate.

The push for a runoff amendment extended back to 1930. The success of Act 38 had sidetracked the effort, momentarily, but the legislative reversal in 1935—plus further public outcry over the nomination of Carl E. Bailey for governor in the 1936 Democratic primary by less than 32 percent of the vote—renewed public interest in the proposal. To pass a constitutional amendment, proponents needed to gather 18,000 signatures in a petition drive. This they managed to do and, with the press strongly endorsing the reform and without organized opposition, the citizens of Arkansas ratified the runoff amendment during the general election of November 8, 1938—though only narrowly, 63,414 to 56,947.

The freshly minted Amendment 29, Section 5, of the Arkansas Constitution provided: "Only the names of candidates for office nominated by an organized political party at a convention of delegates, *or by a majority of all the votes cast for candidates for the office in a primary election*, or by petition of electors as provided by law shall be placed on the ballots of any election" (emphasis added). Now, though, the constitutional amendment required enabling legislation. This meant going back to a hostile house and senate. The legislators grudgingly passed the enabling acts, but in the next year they proposed their own constitutional amendment—one designed to strike down the dual primary. By then, however, the public had evidently warmed to the idea of a runoff provision; the argument that the principle of majority rule, reflected in the dual-primary system, honored a bedrock principle of democracy seems to have been persuasive. By a 61.5 percent margin, the voters of Arkansas rejected the proposed amendment. Opposition to the runoff grew steadily weaker and, in the 1940s, trailed off into insignificance. The runoff primary had become as much a part of the political landscape in Arkansas as razorback hog hats were in the cultural landscape.

A Renewed Attack on the Arkansas Runoff

These earlier disputes over the runoff had nothing to do with race. During the thirties blacks could not vote in the state's Democratic primary and only Democrats ever won elections, so the effect of runoffs on blacks was not even a consideration. When Arkansas accepted the runoff, fewer than 2 percent of the state's voting-age blacks were registered.[32] Runoff reformers in this interwar era were driven by their belief in a basic democratic tenant: that no nominee should be chosen who had failed to receive a majority of the ballots cast in an election. As Judge Eisele put it: "The history is clear: race was not a factor. In fact, it has been suggested that fear of the power of the Ku Klux Klan may have been a motivating factor for some. But the perceived perversion of democratic principles (where plurality elections were permitted) was the overriding motivating factor." He observed further that to require a majority vote to be nominated was a "bedrock ingredient of democratic political philosophy" and that "[t]he concept of 'majority-rule' dominates our national mind."[33]

Fifty years after the establishment of the second-primary procedure in Arkansas, though, some blacks had become convinced that—regardless of the original intentions of runoff proponents—the white political establishment was preserving the dual-primary rule for the purpose of racial discrimination. To remedy this perceived injustice, the black plaintiffs in the *Whitfield* case aimed to overturn the runoff enabling legislation and, implicitly, to repeal Amendment 29, Section 5, of the Arkansas Constitution.

The "fact situation" on the discriminatory effects of the runoff was stronger in *Whitfield* than in *Butts*. In New York City, no black or Hispanic had ever led the field in the first primary only to lose in the runoff. In *Whitfield*, however, the plaintiffs presented evidence that in Phillips County during 1986 and 1988 there were four instances in which a black led the first primary but was defeated in the runoff. In another factual difference, no black had been elected to a countywide office in Phillips County since the turn of the century, whereas several minorities had won boroughwide elections in New York City; moreover, the state of New York had elected a black lieutenant governor.

In pressing their claims of discriminatory intent, the plaintiffs pointed to the 1983 enactment that applied the runoff requirement to municipal elections. This new statute came a few months after a black was chosen mayor of West Memphis with a plurality vote in a multicandidate contest.

Judge Eisele conceded that some legislators may have supported the new law in order to block the election of additional black candidates, but that was "beside the point. We are to deal with the overall legislative intent."[34] The overall intent was, in the judge's view, simply an extension of the now well-established majoritarian rule embodied in the runoff provision to a further set of electoral offices.

Eisele relied heavily on the *Butts v. City of New York* precedent, finding the decision of the U.S. Court of Appeals in this case fully persuasive. At the center of his argument, as with Judges Lumbard and Newman in New York before him, stood the conspicuous obelisk of majority rule. A majority

vote offered the blessings of "validation and credibility and invites acceptance," wrote the Arkansas judge; in contrast, a plurality vote often led to
"lack of acceptance and instability." In his opinion, there were "compelling,
obvious reasons, completely unrelated to race, for states to opt for runoff
elections." Further, he was convinced that black electoral success depended
more on "education and communication"—making black voters more aware
of the importance of the electoral process and actually getting them to cast
their ballots—than on carping about the alleged unfairness of the second-
primary rule.[35]

Besides, Eisele continued, in some Arkansas counties (like Phillips, which
was also a named defendant), blacks constituted a majority of the population.
In such instances, if two or more blacks were to run against one white candidate under a plurality rule, the white might well win as the black community
divided its votes and the white community voted cohesively. Under these conditions, a runoff would offer an advantage to the black community.[36]

The judge went on to suggest that there might be a threshold below which,
as a matter of law, there could be no challenge to the runoff.[37] He speculated
that if the voting-age population of blacks were less than 20 percent of the
total, it would be unreasonable for them to expect to nominate one of their
own candidates in a plurality system in the absence of some white support.
Where blacks are few, they must enter into coalitions with others if they hope
to influence the outcome of elections. Eisele opined further that the runoff
requirement could not be discriminatory in jurisdictions in which blacks constituted more than 45 percent of the voting-age population.

Runoffs, according to Eisele, work to reduce artificial barriers based on
race. At least in Phillips County, where blacks made up 53 percent of the
population (not all of whom were registered to vote), candidates had to attract
support from both races in order to win.[38] If a majority vote were not required
for nomination, candidates might attempt to fashion a plurality from the voters of one race.

Judge Eisele rejected as too speculative the plaintiffs' claim that a black
might receive an initial plurality in an electoral contest if the white vote were
split among multiple candidates but then go on to lose in a head-to-head,
runoff confrontation against a solitary white candidate. Changing the election

rules, he reasoned, could alter the entire dynamics and might result in fewer candidates running in the initial primary.

In the final judgment of the U.S. District Court, Eastern District of Arkansas, "It is considered, ordered and adjudged that the complaint of the plaintiffs be dismissed, and it is hereby, dismissed." The score after the *Butts* and *Whitfield* innings was three judges for the runoff and two against.

The Eighth Circuit Reverses—Then Reinstates—Eisele

In December 1989, on a two-to-one vote, the Eighth Circuit Court of Appeals reversed Judge Eisele's decision that Section 2 was inapplicable to runoff elections. Although the appeals court did agree that no showing of a constitutional violation existed (that is, the plaintiffs had failed to demonstrate an intent to discriminate), it interpreted Section 2 broadly and determined that the runoff provision diluted black political influence in Phillips County. Although the plaintiffs had hoped that their challenge would invalidate runoffs statewide, the appellate decision in *Whitfield* left the runoff intact in seventy-four of the seventy-five counties in Arkansas.[39]

After concluding that runoffs were subject to Section 2, the Eighth Circuit reviewed the evidence on the Totality of Circumstances elements. It determined that the evidence supported a finding of dilution on five of the seven primary factors.[40] The *Whitfield* court distinguished the Arkansas situation from that in New York City, asserting—erroneously—that Arkansas law would not preclude white Republicans from voting in the Democratic runoff against a black first-primary leader. Like New York City statutes, Arkansas law bars participation in a runoff by voters who cast first-primary ballots in the primary of another party.

The appellate court also reviewed evidence on the racial composition of the potential electorate in Phillips County. According to 1980 figures, that county's population was 53 percent black. The court observed, however, that the number of blacks who were of voting age summed to a lesser number, 47 percent, which was insufficient under conditions of rigid racial polarization for a black candidate to poll a majority, especially in light of traditional disparities in black and white registration rates.

In a dissenting opinion, the senior circuit judge accepted that "runoff primaries serve a basic principle of representative government: majority rule." The dissent endorsed the validity of the runoff, unless and until Congress explicitly determined that the procedure was dilutive. The dissent also embraced the assessment of the trial judge that the runoff could provide an incentive for reducing racially polarized voting. Judge Eisele had reasoned that, in the second primary, candidates would campaign to expand their support from the first primary and, in doing so, would have an incentive to develop biracial appeals. Although disappointed in the reversal of the trial court, the assistant attorney general of Arkansas, Tim Humphries, took heart in the narrowness of the Eighth Circuit opinion. Leaving the runoff untouched in all but one county "is a significant victory for us," he concluded.[41]

The plaintiffs, though disheartened by the narrowness of the reversal, claimed to be encouraged as well. Lani Guinier, who had tried the case, characterized the Eighth Circuit outcome as "a historic ruling which will help black Americans to overcome one of the principle obstacles to their political empowerment—majority vote requirements."[42] Now armed with a ruling invalidating the second primary, the Legal Defense Fund of the NAACP announced its intention to challenge runoffs elsewhere in Arkansas and in other states that required a majority vote for nomination.

The plaintiffs' elation proved premature, however. In May 1990, the full panel of the Eighth Circuit reviewed the runoff issue and vacated the earlier two-to-one finding for the plaintiffs. The full panel deadlocked five to five, which reinstated Judge Eisele's trial court decision upholding the runoff. This *en banc* outcome was not accompanied by a full opinion, so we cannot know what factors were weighed by the entire court.

Majority Vote in General Elections

As part of a claim that single-member districts in a portion of Arkansas had been configured so as to dilute minority political influence in the state legislature, a challenge was also filed in 1990 against the majority-vote requirement. In *Jeffers v. Clinton*, a three-judge federal panel upheld the majority-vote requirement for partisan primaries but questioned its fairness when applied to general elections.[43]

As a part of their evidence to show a pattern of intentional discrimination, the plaintiffs highlighted events in three municipalities. In four instances involving three cities, shortly after a black candidate enjoyed success with a plurality rule in place, the state legislature approved statutes requiring a majority rule. Each of the contests was for a nonpartisan office, for which a plurality previously had been sufficient for election. The court concluded that the intent to discriminate was so convincing that future efforts to require a majority vote in general elections must be precleared. Arkansas is not subject to preclearance of changes in its electoral statutes under the provisions of the Voting Rights Act of 1965 or its amendments. The court stopped short of invalidating any existing statutes that required a majority vote for election in municipalities. It simply noted that "whether and to what extent these statutes may continue to be validly applied must be left to a case-by-case determination in the future. . . . If a black candidate leads in the first primary and then is defeated in a runoff [in a municipality] . . . the election may be vulnerable to a strong constitutional challenge."[44]

An inability of several black candidates in the *Whitfield* case to win nomination after leading in the first primary proved insufficient for the Eighth Circuit to find minority-vote dilution, and *Jeffers* failed to invalidate any of Arkansas's runoff *provisions*. So, for the time being at any rate, the runoff method of elections had escaped emasculation by the courts.

Throughout the legal wrangling over the *Butts* case, the empirical evidence provided by both sides on the effects of the runoff provision often conflicted. In the next chapter, we examine some of the issues raised in this important case in the light of fresh data on the results of the runoff rule as it has been long practiced in southern elections.

4

Race and the Runoff

During his bid for the presidency in 1984, Jesse Jackson sought to make the majority-vote requirement the rallying point for a new effort to expand minority voting rights. Some rhetoricians placed the majority-vote requirement on a par with discriminatory techniques, now vanquished, such as the white primary and the poll tax. Probably the most extreme statement made on the topic came from a sociologist who testified as to the discriminatory consequences of runoffs in *Butts v. City of New York*. This expert for the plaintiffs asserted that runoffs were America's apartheid.[1]

Yet, in contrast, one can readily find anecdotal evidence that black candidates have fared well under the runoff rule. In North Carolina in 1990, Harvey Gantt, the former black mayor of Charlotte, bested his white opponent 57 to 43 percent in a Democratic runoff for the U.S. Senate nomination. In Arkansas during the same year, Kenneth ("Muskie") Harris, a black, clobbered a Ku Klux Klan supporter and former member of the American Nazi party in a GOP runoff for the lieutenant gubernatorial nomination. Earlier, in 1983, former U.N. ambassador and congressman Andrew Young placed second in the initial primary for the mayorship of Atlanta but beat a liberal, white state legislator in the runoff.

So who is correct? This chapter brings empirical findings to bear on this debate.

The Evidence of North Carolina and Chicago

The most frequently cited evidence for the alleged discriminatory impact of runoffs comes from a 1982 Democratic congressional primary in North Carolina.

In the initial primary, black state legislator Mickey Michaux polled 44 percent of the vote, which gave him a 12,400 vote lead over Tim Valentine, a white and former chair of the North Carolina Democratic Executive Committee. A second white candidate received the remaining 23 percent of the ballots. In the runoff, Michaux's vote total rose by 2,800 but he still lost to Valentine by a 54 to 46 percent margin. Jesse Jackson seized upon Michaux's inability to expand his plurality and win nomination to illustrate how runoffs thwart black political ambitions.[2] Critics contended that in constituencies where blacks constituted a sizable minority, a black candidate could be the leading vote getter when facing multiple whites; however, if the white vote rallied behind the single white runoff candidate, the black would be denied nomination.

Reinforcing Michaux's experience has been the defeat of two other black candidates in statewide races. In 1978 James Clyburn had a 261-vote lead over one of two white candidates seeking the nomination to become South Carolina's secretary of state. Clyburn's vote total dropped by 8,000 between the primary and the runoff, while his opponent attracted 20,000 additional votes. Similarly, Howard Lee, then mayor of Chapel Hill, North Carolina, held a 2,300-vote lead in an eight-way contest in the 1976 Democratic primary for lieutenant governor. Lee lost the runoff—despite increasing his share of the vote from 27.7 to 43.9 percent. Could it be that runoff reversals for more visible black statewide candidates have been the basis for a black-loses myth, much as statewide contests provided distortions that may have spawned the leader-loses and incumbent-loses myths explored earlier? (Later in this chapter we review the available data on the relationship between race and electoral success in runoffs.)

In contrast to black defeats in runoff states, Jackson could look to his own Chicago and its recent mayoral election for further grist for his mill. Under the city's plurality-vote system for mayor, Harold Washington, a black congressman, won the 1983 Democratic nomination in a fiercely contested three-person field that included white incumbent Jane Byrne and another white, Richard Daley, the son of legendary Mayor Daley. (The younger Daley was elected mayor in 1989 after Washington's death.) Thus, in Chicago a black had succeeded when a plurality sufficed, whereas in North Carolina, Michaux, who received a larger share of the vote than Washington, lost the second primary and failed to become the Democratic nominee.

There is yet a third perspective on the impact of rules governing needed vote shares. How representative of plurality systems was Harold Washington's triumph? We do not pretend to have the data needed for a comprehensive assessment, but consideration of the full range of possibilities dictates inclusion of the following case. In 1984 Katie Hall, who is black, enjoyed the advantages of incumbency as she sought renomination to Congress from Indiana. Hall was challenged by three whites in the Democratic primary in which a plurality would be sufficient. In contrast to Washington, who narrowly eked out a plurality, Hall finished second in a contest where only 4,000 votes separated the top three candidates. There is, not surprisingly, no guarantee that a single minority will win nomination when facing multiple whites, as Hall's inability to capitalize on the advantages of incumbency underscores.[3]

Mississippi attorney Victor McTeer, in testimony before a House Judiciary subcommittee in 1985, expressed the central criticism of the runoff: "Blacks consistently lose runoffs because of historic white racial bloc voting against black candidates." According to McTeer, "When poor black candidates are required to finance two campaigns rather than one, get out the vote twice rather than once, aid and provide illiterate black voters with voting assistance on two occasions rather than one, the resulting drain of finances and other resources makes the dual primary a real threat to equal participation in both party and general electoral politics."[4]

A black member of the Georgia Assembly opposed the runoff rule on similar grounds. "Elections under the runoff provision are like a gun fight at the OK-Corral," complained Democrat Michael Thurmond. "By the time you shoot your way through the first election, you're all out of ammunition—with another election to go just for the nomination!"[5] (Though Thurmond participated in a runoff in his first bid for the legislature, he was not disadvantaged by the majority-vote requirement, having placed second in both rounds.)

The Disincentive Thesis

An additional consideration is whether the need for a majority of the vote to be nominated may dissuade potentially electable blacks. As with white can-

didates, risk taking among black candidates is conditioned by their estimate
of how they will perform. It has been suggested that some blacks who might
expect to win a plurality would not run if they doubted they could garner a
majority. "The majority-vote requirement's disincentive effect is immeasur-
able," writes William Simpson. "Thus, the real inquiry concerns the existence, not the extent of the racially discriminatory impact." As evidence of
the runoff's disincentive effect, Simpson observes: "Most states requiring
runoffs have not elected blacks to Congress or to statewide office since
disenfranchisement."[6]

Although Simpson is accurate that black candidates have not performed
well in congressional and statewide contests in runoff states, it should be
noted that blacks have won relatively few of these elections even in nonrunoff
states.[7] It is true that a greater number of black members of Congress have
been elected from states without a runoff; however, in both runoff and nonrunoff states, election to the U.S. House of Representatives seems to hinge
primarily on the existence of a majority black district. Lindy Boggs, a Democrat from New Orleans, was the last white representative from a majority
black district anywhere in the nation when she chose not to seek reelection in
1990. Georgia, Louisiana, Mississippi, and Texas—all runoff states—have
elected blacks to Congress from majority black districts. Outside of the
South, blacks have been elected from eleven states, with all majority-black
districts selecting African American representatives. Few have won in districts that did not have a black majority.[8]

Those who argue the disincentive thesis choose to alter one aspect of
the status quo while assuming that all other features will remain unchanged.
In doing so, they are not alone; Jesse Jackson and others seem to believe
that elimination of the majority-vote requirement would have no impact on
candidate recruitment or voter behavior. Yet, if the share of the vote needed
for nomination were to be modified, it is far from clear what the results
might be.

To illustrate, one consequence might be a decline in the number of serious
contestants. Individuals who acknowledge that they would probably not be
the front-runner in a plurality system might still enter a multicandidate field
in a majority-vote system if they thought they could finish second and that the

front-runner would not garner a majority. For example, Zell Miller, who relied on blacks, teachers, and urbanites to challenge Senator Herman Talmadge
(D-Ga.) in the 1980 Democratic primary, explained: "I hope that coalition
will get me into the runoff." [9] Under a plurality rule, which gives a candidate
one time at bat to hit a home run or strike out, prospective second-place
finishers have less incentive to run. If the number of serious white candidates
declined following a change to plurality elections, there would be fewer situations where a black candidate might hope for nomination—in a crowded
field—with no more than a plurality of the vote provided by black supporters.
A de facto majority-vote requirement would remain if eliminating runoffs led
to fewer situations where a single black opposed multiple white candidates
and to more instances where one strong white candidate opposed a black
candidate.

Taking this line of reasoning a step further, Harold Stanley has suggested
that, if those who believe the runoff to be racist or racist-inspired are correct,
then racist whites will carefully map a strategy to settle on a single white to
deny the nomination to a black candidate. Civil rights attorney Laughlin
McDonald cites a particularly clear instance of white action to ensure unity
against a black opponent. When a black challenged two whites for election in
the small town of Thomson, Georgia, the white candidates met to determine
which one would drop out. The candidate who was to drop out reneged, at
which point the other candidate announced that he was giving up his campaign even though he had been betrayed by the other white. The overt goal was
to ensure that a black would not triumph as a result of a split in the white vote. [10]

Even if the adoption of a plurality rule for nomination failed to produce
fewer candidates, it might influence the voting choices of some voters. In
crowded fields under a majority-vote rule, some voters will support their
most-preferred candidate in the initial balloting, even if they foresee little
likelihood of this individual winning. The voter does this in the expectation
of a second primary, in which it will be possible to support the successful
candidate. Without the possibility of a second primary, a larger share of the
electorate is likely to line up behind one of the top two candidates rather than
waste a vote on a contender who has little prospect of prevailing in the primary. In support of this proposition, Bradley Canon has shown that plurality

states tend to have fewer serious candidates—defined in terms of the share of the vote received—than do states in which a runoff is possible.[11]

Canon's analysis of vote distributions in gubernatorial elections has been reinforced by at least one study of local elections. Based on an analysis of voting patterns in Sumter County, South Carolina, Morgan Kousser concluded that the voting behavior of whites changed in the face of serious black challenges. Even when a majority vote was required, Kousser dubbed the winnowing of preferences by the white electorate before the initial vote "a psychological white primary."[12]

Another factor that has received little attention from majority-vote critics is the potentially benign impact of the runoff on black candidates in heavily black political units. The logic that argues that, in the context of racially polarized voting, blacks are disadvantaged in white areas also supports the proposition that runoffs handicap white candidates in predominantly black areas. Multiple blacks could split African American support in black areas, allowing a white to win a plurality, just as a single black could run ahead of competing whites in a majority-white constituency. Andrew Young has warned that "without a runoff it's much less likely that a black could be elected mayor of Atlanta, because a single white candidate would be able to win a plurality of votes in a primary against a divided black field." Hosea Williams, a leader in Jesse Jackson's 1984 campaign in Georgia, changed his stance and advocated the majority vote when he became one of four blacks challenging white congressman Wyche Fowler.[13]

Perhaps it is this two-edged sword aspect of the runoff, coupled with the possible decline in the number of serious candidacies, that prompted Laughlin McDonald, an experienced voting rights attorney, to conclude: "[D]espite the discriminatory aspect of the majority vote requirement, it is doubtful that its abolition would have a beneficial impact." Elsewhere, McDonald summed up his views on the pros and cons of eliminating the runoff: "The effect of the abolition of the majority vote requirement would (1) be minimized by the ability of the white community to choose consensus candidates prior to the general election, and (2) deprive majority black jurisdictions of the protection which the majority vote requirement bestows upon them. On balance, however, the requirement no doubt does more harm than good."[14]

Federal Law and the Runoff

The Justice Department has considered the majority-vote requirement a possible violation of the 1965 Voting Rights Act. Particularly suspect have been jurisdictions subject to the Section 5 preclearance requirement of the law. This provision prohibits certain jurisdictions from changing their electoral laws without first securing the approval of the Justice Department or the federal district court sitting in the District of Columbia. Denial of preclearance is especially likely in jurisdictions that have sought to change from a plurality- to a majority-vote rule. Between 1965 and 1981, there were eighty instances in which a majority-vote requirement was one of the items cited by the Justice Department when rejecting a proposed change.[15]

More recently, the 1982 amendments to the Voting Rights Act strengthened what had been an inconsequential portion of the legislation. Legislators modified Section 2 of the law to eliminate any need for minorities to prove a discriminatory intent in order to successfully challenge an existing electoral provision; all that plaintiffs must show now is that the challenged provision has an unequal impact on minorities. At the same time that it adopted the "results" or "effects" standard in place of an "intent" test, Congress went on record to oppose a requirement that minorities be represented on governing bodies in proportion to their share of the population (proportional representation).

In trying to help the courts chart a course between these seemingly conflicting standards, Congress identified seven conditions to be weighed in determining whether the totality of circumstances indicates the existence of minority-vote dilution (see chapter 3, "Rejection of the Runoff Rule"). Among the seven conditions is a collection of enhancement factors, one of which is the majority-vote requirement. The 1982 legislation by no means bars runoffs, but it does question their fairness.

Even though Congress has not banned runoffs, the Justice Department took aim at the majority-vote requirement in 1990. In August, the attorney general of the United States filed suit challenging the use of runoffs in Georgia. The primary emphasis of this suit seems to have been that maintenance of the runoff is discriminatory in its effects, regardless of the intent behind its adoption. During the fall of 1990, the assistant attorney general responsible for civil rights indicated that eliminating the majority-vote requirement was one of the top goals of the Bush administration. A few months later the Justice Department sued the city of Memphis, Tennessee, for that purpose.

As discussed earlier, some observers believe this challenge to the majority-vote requirement is politically motivated. Their assumption is that disrupting activities in the Democratic party may advantage the GOP. A number of Democratic officeholders have warned that if elimination of the runoff resulted in black Democrats being nominated with pluralities, these nominees would likely face defeat in the general election.

An Intent to Discriminate?

A Range of Opinions

Although Section 2 of the Voting Rights Act obviates the need to prove a discriminatory intent in adopting or maintaining a dual-primary system, some attorneys and historians perceive intentional racism at work. Attorney Victor McTeer, for example, sees the runoff as "one of the oldest guarantees of southern white political domination." Historian Morgan Kousser asserts that the runoff was adopted as a further guarantee that blacks would be unable to influence southern elections. Kousser's views on the runoff have been echoed by Laughlin McDonald of the American Civil Liberties Union (ACLU): "The majority vote requirement has its roots in nineteenth century southern white racism, and it frequently operates today to dilute the voting strength of blacks." [16]

Peyton McCrary, the Justice Department's in-house historian, has often concluded that adoption of the majority-vote requirement was racially motivated. He has argued that even if there were few black voters, the runoff had a racial intent because it was embraced with a desire to dilute black influence in the event that blacks registered in sizable numbers. Despite the claims by McCrary and others, William Simpson, who reviewed the work of historians and political scientists on the origins of the runoff, concluded: "Proof of purposeful discrimination in the adoption of second primaries presents an elusive target." [17]

In an article published in 1944, shortly after Arkansas became one of the last states to adopt the runoff, Henry Alexander saw no evidence that this change was instituted to weaken black political influence. Rather, a motivation of Arkansas runoff supporters was the desire to weaken Klan influence on the Democratic party primary system. Nonetheless, Alexander speculated that if blacks were to become active in Democratic party politics following the demise of the white primary, runoffs "might become a bulwark of 'white supremacy' by consolidating the much larger voting strength of the white population." [18]

The allegation of discriminatory intent is challenged by individuals who note that by the time a majority-vote requirement was adopted in the South, most states already had in place other disfranchising techniques such as the poll tax, literacy tests, or a white primary, which had removed most blacks from the voting lists. Further, when techniques like the white primary or literacy tests were invalidated, white political leaders were not heard to boast that white supremacy was safe so long as the majority-vote requirement prevailed. [19] Rather, virtually no commentators writing prior to the mid-1980s said that the runoff seriously devalued black political influence. [20] Those who now see an intent to discriminate against blacks also ignore the fact that when runoffs were being adopted, the loyalty of many southern blacks was to the GOP, not the dominant Democratic party.

An alternative explanation is that southern states adopted the runoff in the wake of the demise of the Republican and Populist parties, which left most of the South dominated by a single party. With a single party and with nominee selection passing from conventions to primaries, the runoff ensured that officeholders had obtained majority support on at least one occasion. Similarly, the Citizens Union Foundation has observed that "runoff elections are based on the sound principle that persons elected to represent the public should have the substantial support of the public. Runoffs allow the wishes of the electorate to be more clearly expressed." A *New York Times* editorial made the same point: "No theory or value of government should require a party to create a free-for-all lottery election just to satisfy the long-shot hopes of some of its members, and no candidate should want the burden of having to govern with a lesser mandate." [21]

Political scientist Lorn Foster treads the middle ground, speculating that "runoff primaries were probably intended both to facilitate intra-party competition and to exclude blacks." [22] Regardless of the reasons for establishing the runoff, Foster endorses the idea that the runoff is colorblind and does not disadvantage any minority group in a party. He claims, however, that because there are relatively few majority-black jurisdictions, blacks are infrequently advantaged by the majority-vote requirement.

Michaux Multiplied?

Most critics see the dilutive effects of runoffs on black political aspirations as wide-ranging. Peyton McCrary, however, focuses on the juxtaposition of multiple factors: at-large elections for multimember legislative bodies in conjunction with a sizable black population and a majority-vote requirement. As he puts it: "Generally speaking[,] in communities where there is a significant black minority and where blacks are registered to a significant degree, the at-large election structure is normally enhanced in its discriminatory impact by the use of a majority-vote requirement. The same does not apply when looking at statewide elections or when looking at most congressional districts, at least not as a general rule." [23]

Laughlin McDonald agrees with McCrary that runoffs become dilutive only under certain circumstances, that is, when applied to at-large elections for multimember bodies. In testimony before a U.S. House subcommittee, McDonald stated:

> The critical problem I believe in most of these jurisdictions is the at-large system. It is generally coupled with a majority vote requirement and the complaints we file always allege that the at-large system delutes [*sic*] and the majority vote system enhances dilution. . . . But where you get rid of the at-large system, then our experience has been that the objection to the majority vote requirement and staggered terms evaporates. They no longer are discriminatory devices because you have a basic system of elections utilizing single member districts that cures their dilutive effect.

In jurisdictions having fairly drawn, single-member districts, McDonald wants to retain a majority-vote requirement. He testified that, "if we get single-member district reapportionment plans, we also want to keep the majority vote requirement because it is a benefit to blacks in the majority black districts." [24]

Steve Suitts, executive director of the Southern Regional Council, agrees with McDonald that runoffs are not discriminatory once single-member districts have been drawn to correct for at-large systems that may have had the effect of disadvantaging blacks. Thus, the runoff may no longer be a hurdle for lesser offices, which brings Suitts to the opposite conclusion of that reached by McCrary. According to Suitts, "The effect of the run-off across the South is probably racially discriminatory in state elections and in congressional elections." [25]

Obviously, runoff opponents disagree over whether the practice is always discriminatory (seemingly Jesse Jackson's stand), discriminatory only for collegial bodies elected at-large (Foster, McCrary, and McDonald), or primarily dilutive for statewide and congressional offices (Suitts). There is also debate over whether eliminating the runoff would result in the election of numerous blacks (Jackson) or have little impact on the racial makeup of public officials (McDonald and Suitts). [26] Speculation about the causes and consequences of the runoff has been far more extensive than quantitative analyses on the impact of the second primary on black candidates. At the heart of this debate lies a central question: Is the Michaux experience common or atypical?

If runoffs do disadvantage blacks, then we would expect to see black first-primary leaders winning nomination in the second primary less often than white first-primary leaders. As shown in earlier chapters, approximately one-third of all first-primary leaders failed to win nomination. Further, chapter 2 reported that the percentage of conversions from a first-primary lead to a runoff victory for candidates in male-female contests differed from that in all-male contests. Particularly during the 1980s, however, front-running women were about as successful in winning nomination as men who had won a plurality against a woman in the initial election. Therefore, even if there were differences in the overall rate of nomination among first-primary leaders in black-white contests (compared with all-white contests), if black and white front-runners were now equally successful, this would mitigate against the finding of potential minority-vote dilution.

The Data on Runoff Impact

The chief obstacle to evaluating the impact of runoffs on black candidates is the difficulty in obtaining a good sample. The *National Roster of Black Elected Officials*, published annually by the Joint Center for Political Studies, has provided lists for successful black candidates since the early 1970s, but there is no comparable listing of unsuccessful black candidates. Moreover, the anecdotal evidence on the impediments caused by the dual-primary system has invariably identified blacks who were defeated in the second primary after leading in the first.[27] To identify congressional runoffs in which blacks competed, we reviewed relevant issues of the *Congressional Quarterly Weekly Report*, the *Almanac of American Politics*, and *Politics in America*. We also turned to political scientists interested in state politics in each of the runoff states for the names of black runoff competitors in contests for the state legislature and higher offices. Finally, we examined *Newsbank* for articles on state legislative runoffs. We suspect that, despite these efforts, we may have missed some black candidates, particularly in earlier years.

Our assessment of the minority-loses myth in this chapter involves three sources of information. First, we review studies of the relationship between black municipal officeholders and the majority-vote requirement. Second, we analyze the elections in our data set for which we have been able to identify black candidates. And third, we draw upon a separate study of black and white runoff success for local offices in Georgia.

The Findings: Race and Runoff Success

Election of Blacks in Municipalities

The Bullock and MacManus study of almost a thousand cities with a 1980 population in excess of 25,000 found that, nationwide, there was little difference between plurality and majority-vote systems and the rate at which blacks were elected to city councils.[28] Differences were greatest in the West and Midwest, but in both of those regions, blacks were slightly *more* likely to serve in cities with a majority-vote requirement. These differences are so slight, however, that it is reasonable to conclude that they indicate no relationship between the share of the vote needed and the incidence of black council members. In the South, where it would seem most likely that a second primary would have a negative effect on black candidates, there was a slight and nonsignificant advantage associated with the use of a plurality system. The frequency with which black councillors were found in cities was not related to the type of election rule employed.

In a second study Ester Fuchs reports on research by the Citizens Union Foundation, which concluded that runoffs did not disadvantage minority mayoral candidates in large cities.[29] Minority candidates won six out of ten runoffs, including two in which the minority candidate rebounded from a second-place finish in the initial primary. In all ten pairs of elections, the minority candidate attracted more votes in the second than the first contest. Of the elections studied, black Democrat Tom Bradley's 1969 fall from plurality leader to runoff loser in Los Angeles was the only example supporting the minority-loses myth. In seven of the ten pairs, the minority candidate finished in the same order in both elections. In major cities, then, the majority-vote requirement appears to be, at most, a flimsy obstacle to the election of blacks.

Beyond the Municipalities

The success rates of primary leaders in state and federal offices (both legislative and executive) are presented in Table 4.1, controlling for the candidates' race. Not surprisingly, the percentages for all-white runoffs are very similar to those presented in chapter 2 for the entire data set. In the second row of Table 4.1, the figures show that in runoffs with black and white candidates, the overall success rate of the primary leader approximates that for all-white runoffs. But these percentages mask a substantial difference concerning the race of the candidate leading the initial primary. Black primary leaders won nomination in nine out of eighteen contests. This stands in stark contrast with

Table 4.1 Success Rate of Primary Leaders in Runoffs,
Controlling for Race, 1970–1986

	Primary Leaders		
Race of Runoff Candidates	Won	Lost	N
All white	70.0%	30.0%	1,162
Black and white	71.1	28.9	38
Black led primary	50.0	50.0	18
White led primary	90.0	10.0	20
All black	71.4	28.6	21

Note: In one runoff won by a black we were unable to determine the race of the candidate who lost.

white primary leaders, who won all but two of the twenty runoffs in which they participated. Finally, Table 4.1 shows that in all-black runoffs, primary leaders were nominated at about the same rate as primary leaders in all-white runoffs. The data in this table support Jesse Jackson's allegations, although some alternative explanations remain to be examined.

Perhaps the low success rate for black primary leaders stems from relatively weak performances in the initial primary; yet the data fail to support that hypothesis. Of nine blacks who polled 40 percent in the initial primary and led the runoff by at least five points, only four were nominated. This success rate of 44.4 percent is substantially below that for all primary leaders with strong initial performances, 80 percent of whom were nominated. The success of blacks who ran well in the first primary is also below that of whites who performed equally well in the first primary against a black second-place finisher. Fifteen of the seventeen whites who came out of the primary with a substantial lead went on to defeat their black opponent in the runoff.

A second alternative explanation would be supported if the poor performance of black primary leaders were attributable to their having contested high-level offices for which primary leaders often encounter difficulties. This proposition is also unsustainable, as only two of the black primary leaders were running for statewide offices; though both of these black candidates

(James Clyburn and Howard Lee) lost, there remain seven other black primary leaders who also came up short in the runoff—even though they sought lesser offices.

Another possibility is that the defeats of black primary front-runners occurred in the 1970s and that black primary leaders fared better in the 1980s. The small number of cases for which data are available show a tendency for black primary leaders to be more successful in the 1980s than in the 1970s. Two out of six black primary leaders were nominated in the 1970s, compared with a seven-for-twelve success rate for the more recent period.

The number of black-versus-white runoffs for higher offices in this data set remains small. It is unreasonable, therefore, to attempt a multivariate analysis in order to disentangle possible explanators, as is possible with the county-level data to be discussed next.

Black and White Runoffs for County Offices

The most extensive study of black-versus-white runoffs has used a data set compiled by Charles Bullock and A. Brock Smith from Georgia counties with sizable black populations. The data come from the sixty Georgia counties that were at least 35 percent black in 1980, or that were less than 35 percent black but boasted a county seat of at least 10,000 people of whom 35 percent or more were black. The period covered is 1970 to 1984. By a careful review of the county newspaper of record, augmented by interviews with knowledgeable local officials and residents, seventy-three runoffs were identified in which a black faced a white.[30]

The overall success rate for front-runners was similar to what we have observed for the basic data set used in this book. In 67.1 percent of the biracial contests, voters nominated the front-runner. However, once controls are introduced for the race of the primary leader, a difference emerges (see Table 4.2) that is similar to the difference displayed in Table 4.1. In half of the contests in which a black led, the primary leader was nominated; in contrast, when a white led a black in the initial primary, the white was nominated 83.8 percent of the time.

Table 4.2 Success Rate of Primary Leaders in Local Georgia Runoffs, Controlling for the Presence of a Black Candidate, 1970–1984

	Primary Leaders	
Race of Runoff Candidates	%	N
All contests	71.3	401
Candidates both white	72.7	315
One white-one black candidate	67.1	73
Black led primary	50.0	36
White led primary	83.8	37
Candidates both black	61.5	13

Source: Charles S. Bullock III and A. Brock Smith, "Black Success in Local Runoff Elections," *Journal of Politics* 52 (November 1990): 1212.

Unlike the experience for higher offices reported in Table 4.1, blacks seeking county office who had sizable primary margins (that is, they polled at least 40 percent of the vote with a five-point lead over the runner-up) were quite successful. Black primary leaders who displayed initial strength were nominated more than three-fourths of the time, a rate slightly above that for all-white runoffs reported in Table 4.1. Blacks who had less convincing leads in the first primary, though, were particularly vulnerable. Of the black primary leaders who received less than 40 percent of the vote and/or led their white opponent by less than five percentage points, only one-fourth were nominated.

The success of blacks with strong initial performances was similar to, although somewhat lower than, the rate for whites who opposed a black runner-up in the second primary. Almost 90 percent of the whites who performed well in the first primary were nominated. There was relatively little difference among white primary leaders based on their initial performance, with 80 percent of the whites who had less convincing leads in the first primary nonetheless winning nomination in the second.

A bivariate analysis suggested the presence of a temporal dimension in runoff performance. When the fourteen-year period was dichotomized at its midpoint, black primary leaders did significantly better in the second half. From 1978 to 1984, 71.4 percent of the black primary leaders were nominated, compared with only 20 percent of those who led primaries in the first seven years.

The proportion of black constituents was not consistently related to the success of black runoff competitors. Only in districts at least 65 percent black was the black candidate clearly advantaged. Black primary leaders won three-fourths of the nominations when the district was 65 percent or more black. In less heavily black constituencies, black front-runners defeated whites less consistently. The rate of black front-runner success was 45.5 percent in districts that were less than half black and in districts that were 50 to 55 percent black. Where the population was 55 to 65 percent black, black primary leaders were nominated 20 percent of the time.

A multivariate logit model correctly predicted all cases for black primary leaders. The variables included in the model were the size of the plurality margin in the initial primary, a dichotomous variable for whether the runoff occurred after 1977, and the per capita income in the county. Blacks were more likely to be nominated when they had larger primary margins, came from more affluent counties, and sought office after 1977.

The Bullock and Smith findings are at variance with runoff results in Mississippi compiled by the Justice Department and mentioned in U.S. House oversight hearings. Civil rights attorney Armand Derfner reports that in approximately one hundred instances, a black who led the initial primary lost the runoff to a white, whereas only once did a white plurality leader lose to a black in the runoff.[31] We were unable to obtain the Mississippi data from the Justice Department, which, reportedly, was unable to locate these files.

Race and Runoff Success

The various findings reviewed here produce different answers to the question of whether the majority-vote requirement disadvantages blacks. The election results from municipalities reveal no evidence of vote dilution; blacks were as likely to serve on city councils in majority-vote cities as in plurality cities. An analysis of election results from Georgia counties suggests that although black primary leaders were disadvantaged in the past, the disparity has attenuated. Nevertheless, a racial disadvantage existed for black primary leaders with weak leads. These individuals are more likely to fail in the second primary than whites who posted similarly weak initial leads. Blacks who had sizable advantages in the initial primary, as well as those who competed in more recent years, are about as likely to win nomination as comparable white primary leaders.

The strongest evidence of a disadvantage for black candidates in the runoff comes from the data set for legislative and executive offices at the state and federal levels. In these cases (the major source of data analyzed in this chapter), none of the alternative explanations for the disparity between black and white primary leaders was supported. We can but speculate that there has been a growing acceptance by white voters of black candidates at the local level but not for higher offices. The size of the constituency and the concomitant difficulty of establishing more personal ties with voters might explain the lower success rates of black candidates at the higher levels. In the same vein, the significance of the position (and the limited number of black candidates who, for the present, may be perceived by white voters as experienced enough for high office) might account for the seemingly greater obstacle posed by the runoff for blacks seeking higher offices rather than local positions.

It is possible that the different election patterns arise from the use of a single state (Georgia) for the county-level analysis, whereas ten states contributed to the data set on runoffs for higher offices. It is conceivable that the Georgia electorate is more tolerant than voters in other states, although many would not accept that proposition without better evidence and we do not urge the point. There is no reason why this should be the case—except that, recently, Atlanta has had two black mayors, Andrew Young and Maynard Jackson, who have been considered effective by both white and black opinion leaders.[32]

Wrestling with the question of possible racial bias in state elections (and concerned about alienating black voter support), North Carolina Democrats have experimented with submajority thresholds as a new wrinkle in the runoff. Our next chapter explores the ramifications of these attempts to modify more traditional runoff rules.

5 The North Carolina "Threshold" Experiment

In 1989 North Carolina became the first state since Louisiana to modify its runoff provision. Whereas the changes taken by Louisiana in 1975 created a nonpartisan initial primary for all comers (with a second election required if no one received a majority), the North Carolina changes established a threshold for nomination but at a level below 50 percent of the vote.

The North Carolina law was somewhat different from that of other states in that it provided for the right to demand a second primary when no candidate received a majority. The legislation replaced the majority requirement with a stipulation that the primary leader had to garner a "substantial plurality" in order to avoid the possibility of a second primary. The legislation defined substantial plurality as 40 percent of the vote cast for an office. The 40 percent cutoff was already in place in New York City and had been suggested (though not yet adopted) for South Carolina as well.

Black legislators in North Carolina had sponsored proposals to eliminate the runoff as early as 1973. Prior to 1989, none of these proposals had even made it to the floor for a vote. Instrumental in the positive response accorded the 1989 proposal were several fresh developments. First, the 1988 state Democratic party convention endorsed a proposal to eliminate the runoff procedure. Second, the state board of elections concluded (in September 1988) that the runoff discriminated against blacks. The board lacked authority to eliminate the requirement, however, because runoffs were mandated under state law.

A third factor, and perhaps the most important, was the willingness of the bill's sponsor, Senator Ralph Hunt (a black), to settle for half a loaf in 1989.

After introducing legislation that would have eliminated the runoff altogether, Hunt modified his proposal so that runoffs could still be requested when the primary leader polled less than 40 percent of the vote. This compromise legislation attracted a wider range of support than had earlier proposals designed to abolish the runoff entirely. It also benefited from bipartisan backing. With the state Democratic party on record as favoring the legislation, it became more difficult for Democratic legislators to oppose the initiative. Further, some Democrats may have favored reducing the number of runoffs, as second primaries might provoke bitterness and weaken the party in the approaching general election.[1]

Republicans supported the bill for two reasons. First, they expected that eliminating the runoff would result in the nomination of blacks in the Democratic primary who could more easily be defeated by Republicans in the general election. Second, as some Republican leaders explained, they supported the bill in an effort to win support from black voters and black legislators who believed the majority-vote standard to be discriminatory.[2]

Enactment of the legislation also may reflect the growing power of the Black Caucus in the North Carolina legislature and the black electorate.[3] The caucus lobbied aggressively to save the bill from a purportedly crippling amendment in a House Judiciary subcommittee. Some Democratic legislators with sizable black constituencies, including House Speaker Josephus Mavretic, were caught in a bind. If they opposed the antimajoritarian bill, they would antagonize some black constituents; however, by approving the legislation, they opened the door for a potential black primary victory should they be challenged simultaneously by one or more white candidates and a black candidate.[4] Caucus leader Mickey Michaux explained that some cross-pressured Democrats facilitated enactment by absenting themselves from the chamber when the final roll call was taken.[5]

The Threshold Debate

In Favor of a Threshold

Proponents of the 1989 legislation, led by Senator Hunt and Representative Michaux, argued that the runoff disadvantaged blacks and women. Hunt claimed that blacks "consider the second primary as somewhat of a residue of the old slave process. . . . [It] is one of the vestiges that impedes the process of blacks becoming major players in the mainstream of politics." [6]

An increase in the nominations of black and female candidates was only one advantage envisioned by supporters. Backers of the bill pointed to the lower turnout often experienced in runoffs as a reason to have the nomination decision made in the initial primary. They also presented evidence on the expenses associated with a second primary. The director of the legislature's drafting division estimated that a single statewide runoff in North Carolina cost the state between $800,000 and $900,000. [7]

Another argument against the majority-vote requirement emphasized the changing nature of North Carolina politics. With Republicans controlling the governorship and one U.S. Senate seat, as well as being part of a bipartisan coalition that elected the House Speaker in 1989, the state was no longer the one-party entity that had adopted the majority-vote requirement in 1915. With a growing GOP, general elections in North Carolina were frequently contested; thus, if the Democratic party were to nominate a candidate from a splinter faction, that person might be defeated in the general election. [8] Representative Michaux hoped that without a second primary, the Democratic party—realizing the threat posed by the GOP—might coalesce more tightly around its nominee. [9]

Opposed to a Threshold

In response to these arguments, opponents of the proposed change pointed to the value of a majority-vote rule. They advanced many of the same positions embraced by early proponents of the runoff, particularly the advantages of nominating a candidate with the backing of a majority of the party's voters. They also worried about the partisan consequences of lowering the threshold for nomination. While the house majority leader believed that eliminating the runoff would "devastate both parties," a larger number of Democrats saw the legislation as harmful only to their party. [10]

Legislators from heavily black counties in the eastern part of the state were the strongest opponents of change. According to one former legislator, "You will take those areas in Eastern North Carolina that have a high black population and because of the race issue, they will elect a black in the primary and a Republican in the fall, and they will do it consistently. They will do it for race. That is a sad commentary, but that is a fact of life." [11]

Adoption of a Runoff Threshold

Eventually, overwhelming majorities in both chambers supported the threshold reform. The senate, which had originated the legislation, acted first, and the house followed several months later. As predicted by North Carolina political pundits, most of the opposition came from legislators representing the eastern counties.

The most serious challenge to the legislation came in the House Judiciary Subcommittee on Election Laws, which approved a modification in the threshold proposal. In place of the 40 percent figure for avoiding a runoff, the subcommittee set the threshold at 45 percent. This prompted the bill's sponsor, Ralph Hunt, to exclaim, "It's not only been gutted, but they cut anything else out of it that may have been a part of the lifeline." [12]

Based on an application of the 40 percent rule to prior North Carolina runoffs, analysts projected that about two-thirds of the potential runoffs would be obviated by the new threshold. [13] (Newspaper accounts provide no comparable figures for what share of the past runoffs would have been necessary had a 45 percent rule been in place.)

Anticipated Results of the New Threshold

Initially, Representative Michaux predicted: "I think you will see the face of politics change." Subsequently, he modified this opinion: "I think it will lead to at least the nomination, and the election, of more blacks and women because they are the ones who have suffered most from the 50 percent [rule] and this gives them the chance." [14] Michaux seemed to hedge his bet, however, by observing further that he did not expect to see a large number of new black or female nominees. In his view, the real significance of the legislation was its attempt "to remove the racial barriers." [15]

Another anticipated result was an advantage for incumbents. In light of their greater name recognition and fund-raising capabilities, incumbents should be able to achieve 40 percent of the vote, reasoned some, even if 50 percent lay beyond their grasp.[16]

A consequence foreseen by some academics, but not widely discussed by the press, was a reduction in the number of candidates. Bradley Canon's research shows that candidate fields tend to be smaller in plurality- than majority-vote states. Harold Stanley has argued that in situations where white Democrats fear that a black could be nominated only to lose the general election, whites will tend to rally behind fewer candidates in hopes that one of the whites will be the leader and thus have a better chance of capturing the nomination.[17]

Of course, changing the rules can change the outcomes in unanticipated ways. Altering the conditions under which one can expect a runoff may alter the calculus of some candidates who, though harboring no illusion that they can lead a crowded field, hope to place second and then attract the support of the also-rans. Also eliminated would be candidates who have no expectation of winning nomination but hope to offer their support to one of the runoff contestants in return for some future benefit.

A claim made by the U.S. Department of Justice when it sued the state of Georgia for maintaining a majority-vote requirement was that this requirement dissuades potential minority candidates. The reasoning behind this claim is that minorities might anticipate being able to finish first in a multicandidate field but do not run when a majority vote is required for nomination. The Justice Department contended that minorities in majority-white jurisdictions can expect to lose the runoff when they confront a single white candidate who will consolidate the white vote. John R. Dunne, head of the department's Civil Rights Division, declared that the runoff would have "a chilling effect on black political participation." Political scientists Lloyd Jones and Lee Johnston similarly hypothesize that replacing the 50 percent requirement with a 40 percent rule will produce greater numbers of black, female, and Republican candidates. Nevertheless, they also speculate that the impact of the change will be so modest that it may go undetected.[18]

Apparently, Dunne believed that removing the majority-vote requirement would not produce a total thaw in black political ambitions. He assumed that while no blacks would run in many contests subject to a runoff, only one black would offer per contest under a plurality rule. If the 50 percent rule has truly stifled black ambition, why not expect more than one black to run if a plurality sufficed? More than one black opposing more than one white might be no more conducive to the nomination of a black than would be a face-off of one black and one white—an alternative consequence of eliminating the runoff. Neither scenario might produce a result different from the status quo.

Some observers anticipated few changes with the implementation of the new statute in North Carolina. Political scientist Thomas Eamon, for example, predicted that the "ethnic impact of it would be limited. You would tend to see a lot of the same people elected as we've had in the past." [19]

Potential Changes in Other States

At this point in the analysis, we examine the potential consequences of changing to a 45 or 40 percent threshold for nomination. Our assessment is based on the 1,222-case data set undergirding the research presented in this volume. We consider the proportion of runoffs that might have been eliminated with a 40 or 45 percent threshold and whether modifying the standard for nomination would have altered the frequency with which front-runners were nominated in the remaining pool. We also evaluate the proposition that fewer incumbents would have been forced into runoffs.

Finally, we look at the data by gender and race to see whether more women and blacks might have been nominated under different threshold standards. But even if the candidates had remained the same, some voters might have responded differently. For example, some voters support a candidate in the initial primary despite the realization that their candidate has little chance of success. In the first primary these voters indulge the choice of their heart; in the runoff they follow their heads. In a plurality system where there is no potential for a second vote, fewer voters will support long shots because they are unwilling to "throw away" their only opportunity to influence the nomination. Another consequence of a change in the rules applies exclusively to a modification of the law, such as in North Carolina where the vote threshold is reduced but not eliminated. With a lower threshold, fewer nominations should be decided in a second primary. Fewer second-primary contests may attract fewer voters back to the polls, which may have an impact on the outcomes. A smaller turnout may benefit the candidate with the stronger organization. This potential consequence, however, is one for which we lack the information necessary to carry out an evaluation.

In light of the several ways discussed above in which a rules change might affect behavior, the following analysis must be seen as speculative and by no means conclusive. Indeed, because we cannot build in the impact of other changes stemming from lowering the nomination threshold, the figures we present are probably more favorable to the reformer's claims than a before-and-after test.

An Assessment of Lower Thresholds for Runoffs

Effect on Runoff Frequency

If nomination becomes possible with smaller percentages of the vote, then there will be fewer instances where a runoff is required to pick the nominee. Of the total number of cases in our data set, under a 45 percent threshold for nomination, runoffs would have been necessary in 924 instances (76 percent). If the new North Carolina standard of 40 percent had been in place, then 584 runoffs (48 percent) would have been necessary. For each drop of five percentage points in the share of the vote needed to nominate, approximately 25 percent of the runoffs would have been obviated.

We anticipated that the reduction in the number of runoffs would not be constant across offices sought. Specifically, runoffs would continue to be more prevalent—even with smaller shares of the vote needed for nomination—for the more desirable offices. A second expectation was that runoffs would continue to be needed when the initial pool of candidates was larger. A third expectation was that, if the vote needed to nominate were reduced, the runoff would continue to be more frequent in the Democratic party than in the GOP. Finally, in light of the advantages associated with incumbency, we expected that lowering thresholds would eliminate more runoffs involving incumbents than for open seats.

In this section we also present data on the consequences of lower thresholds for the nomination of certain kinds of candidates. Given the advantages accruing to incumbents in terms of name recognition, campaign skills, and the ability to raise funds, we would expect that more incumbents are nominated as the share of the vote needed is reduced. Reformers in North Carolina suggest that larger numbers of blacks and women will be nominated if less stringent standards are applied. We test these propositions as well.

Office Sought

Table 5.1 shows the frequency of runoffs that would have been required for our data set under the two alternative thresholds. The first column gives the number of runoffs held under the majority rule (50 percent) for each office surveyed. The second and third columns indicate the proportion of runoffs listed in the first column that would have been required had a 45 or 40 percent rule been adequate for nomination. As an illustration, consider the thirty-two gubernatorial runoffs in our data set. If 45 percent of the vote had been sufficient for nomination (with all other variables held constant), twenty-four, or 75 percent, of the runoffs would have been necessary. With nomination by 40 percent of the vote, eighteen, or 56.3 percent, of the runoffs would have been required.

Our expectation that the need for runoffs would most likely persist for the more desirable offices failed to be consistently supported. While the most desirable offices in our data set were that of governor and U.S. senator, they did not rank first and second in terms of the proportion of runoffs that would have been required with lower-vote thresholds. Lowering the vote thresholds was particularly apt to reduce the need for runoffs in U.S. Senate races.

Using a 45 percent standard for nomination, the fewest runoffs would have been eliminated for the office of lieutenant governor and for lesser, statewide executive officials. For these positions, at least 80 percent of the runoffs would still have been necessary. At a 40 percent standard, the lieutenant governor continues to be the position with the smallest reduction in number of potential runoffs, whereas the governor's office registers the second highest

Table 5.1 Frequency of Runoffs Needed under Alternative
Thresholds for Nomination, by Office

Office	Number of Runoffs under Majority Rule	% of Runoffs Needed under	
		45% Rule	40% Rule
Governorship	32	75.0	56.3
Lt. Governorship	13	84.6	69.2
Other statewide executive offices	30	80.0	53.3
U.S. Senate	24	70.8	45.8
U.S. House	112	70.5	41.1
State Senate	225	71.6	45.8
State House	786	77.6	48.7
Total	1,222	75.8	48.0

number of necessary runoffs. For both the 45 and 40 percent vote standard, the greatest number of runoffs would have been eliminated for U.S. House seats.

It seems likely that the post of lieutenant governor experiences such contentious elections because it attracts relatively large fields of candidates, many of whom remain reasonably viable even at the end of the campaign. Locked in a less important and visible contest, candidates for lieutenant governor and cabinet positions generally lack the funding and media attention accorded leading gubernatorial aspirants. Fewer of these candidates may find themselves squeezed out of campaigns than is the case in gubernatorial or senatorial contests. With war chests generally smaller for candidates seeking lesser statewide offices, and with less extensive polling done on these contests, more aspirants may be able to hold on for the duration of the campaign.

Moreover, apparently it is less likely that one or a few candidates for secondary statewide positions will emerge from the pack, as in the case of other posts. Perhaps the lower visibility of minor office seekers makes it difficult for any one of them to obtain at least 45 percent of the vote.

Table 5.1 suggests that one of the advantages prophesied for substituting a

40 percent for a majority-vote requirement will not pay the dividends expected. A supposed benefit of the lower threshold was that by eliminating a share of the runoffs, the state would save money, as fewer elections would be necessary. Yet the fewest runoffs would be eliminated for statewide positions (other than U.S. senator). It makes little difference in cost whether there is one or multiple runoffs statewide, because if any statewide position goes to a runoff, the entire electoral apparatus will have to be mobilized a second time.

The position at issue in the highly publicized Michaux runoff—that is, a U.S. House seat—turns out to be the one for which there would be the greatest reduction in runoffs if lower thresholds were imposed uniformly throughout the South. Based on our data, the new North Carolina statute will have its sharpest effect on U.S. House elections.

Number of Candidates

Table 5.2 conforms to our expectation: the effects of lower-vote thresholds for nomination are indeed most evident when fewer candidates enter the first primary. When the initial field has three candidates, lowering the threshold for nomination to 45 percent of the vote eliminates almost 40 percent of the runoffs. When the threshold for nomination drops to 40 percent, only one-quarter of the runoffs have to be held. The outcome with four candidates in the first primary is less pronounced; 82 percent of the runoffs will still be necessary under a 45-percent threshold rule, and more than half will be required even with a 40 percent threshold for nomination.

When the initial field consists of five or more candidates, dropping the nomination rule to 45 percent still means retaining at least 90 percent of the runoffs. With six or more candidates, even the 40 percent threshold eliminates fewer than 20 percent of the runoffs. With one exception (for both of the alternative threshold standards), a larger share of runoffs will be necessary as the number of initial candidates increases.

Recall that in North Carolina, state senator Ralph Hunt, a reform leader, criticized an amendment (first approved, then withdrawn by a house subcommittee) that would have substituted 45 for 40 percent of the vote needed for nomination. Hunt claimed that the higher threshold would gut the legislation.

Table 5.2 Frequency of Runoffs Needed under Alternative Thresholds
for Nomination, by Number of Candidates in First Primary

Number of Candidates	Number of Runoffs under Majority Rule	% of Runoffs Needed under	
		45% Rule	40% Rule
3	554	61.6	24.2
4	336	82.1	55.4
5	158	91.8	75.3
6	93	95.7	81.7
More than 6	81	92.6	87.7

According to Table 5.2, Hunt's allegation is most accurate with a small field
of candidates. When large fields are present, runoffs will be common even
with a 40 percent threshold. In the smallest possible field for a runoff (three
candidates), even the 45 percent threshold will significantly reduce the number of runoffs; at 40 percent, runoffs are almost eliminated in three-person
contests.

Party

If a reduction in the vote share needed for nomination affected nothing else,
then dropping the threshold to 45 percent of the vote would eliminate one-
quarter of the runoffs in both the Democratic and Republican parties. Lowering the nomination threshold to 40 percent shows a decided partisan difference.
Whereas half the Democratic runoffs would be eliminated by a 40 percent
standard, two-thirds of the GOP runoffs would be unnecessary.

Open Seats versus Incumbency

With a 45 percent threshold, there would be relatively little difference in the
share of runoffs that might be avoided if an incumbent was involved. Lowering the vote share needed by five percentage points would eliminate 32 percent of the runoffs featuring incumbents and 21 percent of those for open
seats. If, however, the North Carolina threshold were adopted, our expecta-

tions might well be met. Runoffs for incumbents would plummet by 63 percent, compared with a 47 percent drop in runoffs for open seats.

Effect on the Nomination of Blacks

Senator Hunt may have been incorrect in his expectation that lowering the share of the vote for nomination to 40 percent would produce additional black nominees. Table 5.3 presents figures from our data set on the bids for nomination by blacks under four possible standards: a 50 percent rule, a 45 percent rule, a 40 percent rule, and a plurality system. It is assumed that changing the share of the vote needed for nomination would have no impact on the size of candidate pools or voter behavior.

The calculations in Table 5.3 support Hunt's claim that a 45 percent standard would have made his efforts ineffectual. Lowering the nominating threshold from 50 to 45 percent would have produced only one additional black nominee. Lowering the threshold to 40 percent, however, would have resulted in only one less black nominee than would have been the case under a plurality system. Again assuming (probably unreasonably) that everything else remained constant, eliminating all vote thresholds would have produced 64 percent more black nominees as prevailed with the majority -vote requirement. (In reviewing this and the next two tables, one must be keep in mind that even when the numbers of successful nominees are similar, greater differences in the identity of the nominees may have occurred. Thus, even if the numbers of black or female nominees do not vary greatly under some alternative nominating rules, there will be some differences in the individuals who have succeeded. This is true because the runoff permits some second-place finishers to win nomination in the runoff and, conversely, thwarts the ambitions of some candidates who led the initial primary but lost the runoff.)

Effect on the Nomination of Women

North Carolina reformers claim that women were also victimized by the majority-vote requirement. The data in Table 5.4 raise doubts about these claims. Lowering the threshold from 50 to 45 percent would have resulted in no additional female nominees, and dropping the threshold to 40 percent would

Table 5.3 Effects of Alternative Runoff Thresholds
on the Nomination of Blacks (N = 38)

Rule for Nomination	Blacks Nominated	
	N	%
50%	11	28.9
45%	12	31.6
40%	17	44.7
Plurality	18	47.4

Table 5.4 Effects of Alternative Runoff Thresholds
on the Nomination of Women (N = 166)

Rule for Nomination	Women Nominated	
	N	%
50%	72	43.4
45%	72	43.4
40%	69	41.6
Plurality	79	47.6

have produced fewer women nominees than at either of the higher levels! This lower success rate using the 40 percent standard stems from the fact that in contests in which the leading candidate polled more than 40 percent of the vote, second-place women were relatively more likely to be nominated than women leaders were to lose. When no candidate got over 40 percent of the vote, women experienced greater net losses. Only by eliminating the primary altogether were more female nominees produced than with a majority vote.

Windfall for the Incumbent

The final proposition is that lowering the standard for nomination will advantage incumbents. As expected, Table 5.5 reveals that as the threshold

Table 5.5 Effects of Alternative Runoff Thresholds
on the Renomination of Incumbents (N = 363)

Rule for Nomination	Incumbents Renominated	
	N	%
50%	203	55.9
45%	220	60.6
40%	244	67.2
Plurality	272	74.9

for nomination is lowered, the proportion of incumbents renominated rises. Under the majority-vote rule, 56 percent of the incumbents who competed in runoffs succeeded. Dropping the vote for nomination to 40 percent would have increased the success rate among incumbents to 67 percent. If a plurality had sufficed, three-quarters of the incumbents would have been returned to office. All incumbents should march under the banner of "Plurality Elections!" Challengers, on the other hand, will find high runoff thresholds attractive.

Perhaps incumbent members of the North Carolina legislature were aware that removing the majority-vote requirement would make their own reelections more secure. The figures disclosed in this chapter suggest that future reformers might, at least when talking to their colleagues, make a different pitch than the one used in North Carolina. Only one of the projected beneficiaries in North Carolina—the black candidate—seems likely to be helped by the new legislation, as lowering the vote standard failed to produce more female nominees. A more accurate and potentially more persuasive argument would be that making first-primary nominations easier will help not only black contenders but also America's predominant political species: white male incumbents.

This message, if believed by legislators, should virtually guarantee majority support for the change. But it is a message that prudent incumbents will be unlikely to publicize, for the media and potential challengers may cry foul at yet more attempts to enhance the security of entrenched officeholders. Indeed, the argument may be stood on its head by opponents of lower thresholds, challenging the proposed reform on the ground that it is largely an incumbent protection plan.

Ironically, if a lower threshold promotes the renomination of incumbents, women and blacks could be the losers. To the extent that more blacks or women win public office, their gains will come at the expense of white males. Because white males predominate in this sphere, any policy that promotes their election diminishes the prospects for greater diversity among officeholders.

Facilitating incumbent reelection could be particularly disadvantageous to minorities in the 1990s. The Justice Department and some federal courts are interpreting the 1982 Voting Rights Act as requiring that districts in which minorities constitute a majority of the voting-age population be drawn whenever possible. A number of these newly configured districts will have white incumbents. The enhanced numbers of minority residents may unleash the political ambitions of minority leaders. The upshot could be a white incumbent who is challenged by multiple minority candidates. The lower the threshold for nomination, the more likely that the incumbents' advantages will bring victory.

1990 Results from North Carolina

Results from the 1990 nominating season in North Carolina have been analyzed by Lloyd P. Jones and W. Lee Johnston of the Political Science Department at the University of North Carolina campus in Wilmington.[20] They compare the 1990 primaries with the primaries of 1988. Typically, there was little competition for nominations in either year. The removal of the majority-vote requirement had an impact on a maximum of five state legislative nominations, which were won with between 40 and 50 percent of the vote. Whites won three of these, while one each went to a black and a Native American. Changing the runoff rule, then, did not result in the nomination of numerous additional minorities.

According to Jones and Johnston, the number of candidates competing for office increased in 1990. More Republicans ran for each of the three posts considered (state house, state senate, and U.S. House), whereas Democratic candidacies increased only for the state house. The increased candidacies resulted from a greater number of contested nominations, however, so that the average number of candidates per contest held constant. Only the state house attracted a larger number of black candidates as well as additional female candidates.

Jones and Johnston do not control for incumbency versus open seats. Nor do they provide information on candidacies for years before 1988; thus, we have no indication whether that year is an appropriate benchmark or whether it may have had an atypically small number of contested primaries. Another potential control that is missing would be a comparison of candidacies in North Carolina with those in other states for the same years. In the absence of these controls, we cannot know whether the increased candidacies reported are attributable to the change in the nominating rule.

The authors are cautious and do not lay the changes to the new threshold for nomination. "In separating the direct effects of the election law change, we find ourselves hard pressed to suggest that it had a significant effect," write Jones and Johnston. "While there were more Republicans, blacks and women in the primary election, the fact that there were so few runoffs in both years suggests that enthusiasms for change were exaggerated by proponents."[21] Indeed, they see the runoff continuing to be a major aid to the Democratic party.

Far more visible than the state legislative primaries analyzed by Jones and Johnston was the 1990 election involving the ever-controversial Republican senator, Jesse Helms. The leading candidate to take on Helms, whose opposition to social programs has led critics to dub him "Senator No," was the black former mayor of Charlotte, Harvey Gantt. In the Democratic primary Gantt narrowly missed the magic 40 percent and failed to persuade his chief opponent to forego a runoff. The lower hurdle was still too high for North Carolina's leading black political figure to clear in a single bound. Nevertheless, he went on to an easy runoff victory and a strong, albeit losing, effort against Helms.

We focus our attention next on the relationship between runoffs and voter participation. Does an "extra inning" tire the voter and send him or her home, or does the excitement of a final contest between two would-be champions bring out the "fans"?

6 Runoffs and Voting Rates

By its very nature, the majority-vote system necessitates two elections that occur in close proximity, with the runoff normally coming one to four weeks after the first primary. The need to vote a second time increases the cost of political participation and, therefore, can sometimes reduce turnout in the second primary. Alternatively, in the still largely one-party South, the second primary has narrowed multicandidate fields to the two most viable candidates, thereby providing an added incentive for voters to return to the polls for the climactic ballot.

Presumably, the supporters of the two candidates who make it into the runoff will try to overcome whatever costs the second election involves and turn out in large numbers for the final effort to achieve victory. Some commentators have even suggested that when there is a large field, a certain percentage of voters will intentionally sit out the initial primary on the assumption that the decisive choice of nominees will come in the runoff. When black turnout in the 1990 Georgia Democratic primary proved disappointing, a black leader with strong ties to Jesse Jackson offered this explanation: "A lot of black voters, I think, felt like the real action was going to be in the runoff. People were just assuming that [black gubernatorial candidate] Andy [Young] had a spot in the runoff."[1]

Sometimes surges in runoff turnout have been attributed to voters eager to defeat a candidate they thought would never make it to the second round. Newspaper coverage of a 1990 race for a superior court judgeship in Georgia provides an example. According to an *Atlanta Constitution* reporter, a black candidate lost in two key rural counties when the turnout rose by more than

20 percent, as "white voters were made aware that a black candidate was running and voted in greater numbers to defeat him."[2]

Conversely, those loyal to candidates eliminated in the first primary may discern so little to distinguish between the two remaining competitors that they walk away from the runoff. The incentive to return to the polls may be particularly weak when the remaining competitors have taken similar stands on the issues and these stands are markedly different from those embraced by the candidates eliminated in the first primary. As pollster Claibourne Darden aptly put it, "How do you get your conservative vote out with two liberal candidates? How do you get them the least bit enthusiastic?"[3] Evidence from elections held in 1990 suggests that the answer to Darden's question is, you don't.

In Alabama and Georgia, where Democratic gubernatorial runoffs usually attract more voters than do first primaries, the pattern was broken when, in each state, the runoff featured the two most liberal candidates from the primary. Even when eliminated candidates endorse one of the survivors, this support may be insufficient to motivate their supporters to rally behind their example and vote in the runoff.

In cataloging the problems with a second primary, Lorn Foster told a House judiciary subcommittee that "turnout usually decreases in run-off elections; in fact, the winning candidate in the second round sometimes occasionally receives fewer votes than the frontrunner did in the first round."[4] To illustrate his point, Foster noted that turnout dropped by 130,000 voters between the 1972 Texas Democratic senatorial primaries; thus, the nominee won with 25,000 fewer ballots than the runoff loser had received in the initial primary. Similarly, a study of North Carolina runoffs prompted Mark Lanier to conclude: "Voter turnout usually declines, sometimes precipitously, in the second primary."[5] In one extreme example, participation in North Carolina's 1968 Republican senatorial election dropped from 132,018 votes in the first primary to 14,550 in the runoff![6] An Atlanta councilman who saw turnout drop from 18 to 11 percent of the registrants between his initial primary and the runoff generalized that "there's always a dropoff between the first election and the runoff primary."[7]

Turnout in an election is the product of multiple forces, including concern over the outcome, media time purchased by the candidates, a perception that the contest will be close, and interest in a particular candidate. These variables have the potential to produce sharp variations in turnout from election to election. A sense of civic duty, which motivates many voters, has been declining gradually, but it is apt to be less a source of fluctuations in turnout than the other variables.

Interest in a candidacy, concern over the outcome, and perceptions that one's vote may make a difference are, at least in part, the result of information made available to voters concerning the election. The media generally gives greater attention to top-of-the-ticket contests, such as governor or senator. Therefore, to the extent that media coverage is a direct or indirect stimulant of turnout, we anticipate that turnout in the first and second primaries will be consistent for the higher offices.

Alternatively, although the media is a particularly important source of information about candidates and the status of their campaigns for offices elected statewide, voters may have more direct sources of information about local contests. Thus, a campaign for a local office—especially one where a large number of voters may know one or more of the candidates or may obtain insights about the campaign through conversations with friends or personal observation—may more often produce approximately the same turnout in the two primaries than would a more distant office where reliance on the media is greater. In a contest for county commissioner or even state legislator, for example, more voters may have firsthand information about the candidates than they would in a statewide runoff contest for a post like attorney general. If overcoming inertia and voting in the second primary is keyed to having personal contact or information about candidates, then competition for local offices (such as the state legislature) may trigger greater participation in the runoff.

Some conditions seem to promise a drop in participation in the second primary. If a contest that requires a second balloting does not involve the same size constituency as the initial primary, then a comparison of turnout rates will almost certainly show a decline. If in the initial primary voters nominate a governor or senator, for instance, but do not provide majority support for all congressional or state executive candidates, it would be highly unlikely for the turnout in the second primary to equal that of the initial primary. Indeed, if the first primary involved all of the statewide contests in, say, Texas, and only one congressional contest was to be decided in the runoff, then even if every registered voter in that congressional district turned out for the runoff, statewide turnout rates would show a precipitous drop.

One can anticipate that the greater the number of contests to be resolved by a runoff, the less likely there will be a drop in participation. A citizen's decision to go to the polls may be keyed to specific contests. Some candidates and issues can provoke especially strong feelings in the minds of voters; others do not. When a voter has only weak preferences in some contests, the names on the ballot become more or less extraneous, holding little or no meaning for the citizen who enters the voting booth to support a particular candidate in a single race.

States using the runoff primary select their statewide officers, for the most part, in off-year elections; only North Carolina elects its governor during presidential elections. In South Carolina, the four-year terms of state senators come up for renewal in the off year. Although most southern state legislators serve two-year terms, the added attraction of statewide contests may produce higher runoff voting than in presidential-year primaries.

The same logic may apply in Louisiana and Mississippi. In these states, election schedules are based neither on off years nor on presidential years. Their statewide and state legislative elections follow a four-year cycle, which, for purposes of this research, began with 1971. We call this the *off-off-year cycle*. The same logic that predicted more runoff participation in off-year elections in other states would anticipate higher turnouts in off-off-year elections in Louisiana and Mississippi than in presidential-year elections.

Another possible explanation for the relationship between the number of contests on the runoff ballot and voter turnout is the political party in which the runoff occurs. Because the GOP is still emerging in the South,[8] it will generally have fewer runoffs than the Democratic party. With fewer candidates competing in Republican runoffs, we would expect turnout declines to appear more often on the Republican side.

In this chapter, we explore the extent to which turnout in the runoff differs from that in the first primary and the reasons for the changes in voter participation. Among the variables considered are the nature of the office being contested, the party in which the nomination struggle occurs, and whether the election takes place in a presidential election or an off year. We also discuss briefly the proposition that the winner of the runoff may receive fewer votes than the primary leader.

The Variables Considered

Visibility of the Office versus Personal Contact

Two hypotheses provide alternative perspectives on the relationship between the office contested and relative turnout in each phase of the dual-primary nomination process. According to the *visibility hypothesis*, runoffs should draw relatively more voters when top-of-the-ticket statewide offices are at stake. In contrast, the *personal contact hypothesis* anticipates greater runoff participation in contests for local offices, where voters have a greater probability of personally knowing and interacting with one or both candidates. This hypothesis predicts less dropoff in runoffs for state legislative and county-level offices than for higher posts such as U.S. senator or representative or statewide positions. (Our analysis does not include county contests.)

The Effects of Party

The central reason southern states adopted the runoff provision for state and national contests was the desire to ensure majoritarianism in the absence of two-party competition.[9] But the growing number of viable Republican candidates in the region has prompted some observers to conclude that the runoff has now outlived its usefulness.[10] When contenders clash in a general election, the winners will—almost always—achieve victory with a majority vote.

One partisan implication warrants special attention: because runoffs have been more common in the Democratic party, the interprimary dropoff rate in voter participation from the first to the second primary should be lower among Democrats than Republicans. Further, if bipartisan competition is making the runoff obsolete, then runoffs in the past should have been more successful in attracting voters than those held recently.

Competitiveness

Other explanations for the variation in runoff turnout emphasize competitiveness. The measures of first-primary competition examined here include two used in earlier chapters: (1) the size of the margin enjoyed by the primary leader, and (2) Merle and Earle Black's dichotomous 40-plus-5 measure (whether the primary leader got 40 percent of the vote and defeated the runner-up by at least five percentage points).[11]

In addition to competitiveness, the success of the preferred candidate in the first primary may stimulate a voter to return to the polls for the runoff. To the extent that the continued presence of a favorite candidate prompts runoff voting, then the share of the vote won by runoff contestants in the first primary should be directly related to the second-primary turnout (or, stated another way, it should be inversely related to dropoff rates in the runoff). Therefore, when runoff contestants received a large share of the total vote in the first primary, runoff participation may approximate or even exceed first-primary voting.

To the extent that a larger number of offices at stake may generate a greater number of contests to attract public attention, we would also expect higher runoff participation rates in off-year and off-off-year elections. In other words, voter dropoff between first and second primaries would be greater in presidential-year elections.

Another aspect of voter participation in second primaries warrants attention: the proposition that blacks and women are disadvantaged by runoffs, as the electorate may be mobilized against them. Comparing the number of voters in the primary and the runoff will allow us to assess this proposition. If more of the electorate voted in runoffs, and if at the same time female and black candidates were defeated, this would support—although not prove—the notion that opponents of female and black candidates become active in the second primary in order to block their nomination.

Another possibility is that supporters of women and blacks seeking public office are mobilized during the second primary and, by turning out in great numbers, elect their preferred candidates. Support for this contingency would come from an increase in participation between the primary and the runoff, coupled with the victory of the female or black candidate. Logically, other possible combinations would suggest that second-primary turnout is unrelated to the success of black or female candidates.

Two measures are used to assess changes in participation between the first and second primaries. One of these is the proportion of elections in which more votes were cast in the runoff than in the first primary. The data come from the total number of votes cast for the office involved in the runoff. If runoffs usually attract fewer voters than first primaries, then less than half of the pairs of elections surveyed would have more participation in the runoff.

The second measure of change is the ratio of votes cast in the runoff to votes tallied in the first primary for a particular office. If runoff and first-primary participation tends to be equal, then there would be about as many votes cast in the two sets of elections. This would show up as a score approximating 100 percent; that is, the runoff vote would, on average, equal the first-primary vote. The farther the figure falls below 100 percent, the lower is the average runoff vote compared to participation in the first primary.

The results for individual states from an earlier generation of research are inconsistent. In Alabama during the first four decades of this century, turnout generally decreased between the first and second primaries.[12] After Arkansas adopted a majority-vote requirement, runoff participation exceeded that of the initial primary. In 1942 almost 50,000 more votes were tallied in the runoff, and in 1944 participation rose by almost 17,000 voters between the two primaries.[13] The higher turnout in Arkansas runoffs may well have been attributable to the practice of scheduling elections for which there were only two candidates on the same date as the runoff; thus, the initial Arkansas primary was restricted to contests for which three or more candidates had filed. Unlike in most double-primary jurisdictions, in Arkansas a greater range of decisions could be made in the second primary. With many county offices drawing no more than two contestants—and with these being of particular concern to some voters—the initial primary stimulated less interest.

The Findings

Status of the Office Contested

Our data reveal that two-thirds of the time fewer voters participated in the runoff than in the initial primary (see Table 6.1). A drop in runoff participation (our first dependent variable) was particularly likely in contests for lesser statewide offices, where participation rose in fewer than 10 percent of the runoffs, and for U.S. House contests. In the latter case, voting declined in 84 percent of the runoffs; in senatorial contests, it fell 79 percent of the time. Participation dropped least often in the runoffs for the state house; but, even there, fewer voters participated in the runoff 62 percent of the time.

Results using the second dependent variable (runoff votes cast as a percentage of primary votes cast) do not correspond perfectly with those obtained from the first dependent variable. At the extremes, however, the two are similar: both indicate that contests for lesser state executive positions and the U.S. House were least able to draw voters to the runoff, whereas the typical state house runoff attracted almost 96 percent as many voters as the primary that preceded it. Table 6.1 shows that the major disparity in the two participation measures involves runoffs for U.S. Senate seats. Average voting demonstrates relatively high similarity from first to second primary, with almost 90 percent of the opening primary vote being tallied in the runoff. This is higher than we expected, as only one in five of the U.S. Senate runoffs attracted more voters than their corresponding primary.

The average runoff vote of about 92 percent for governors is slightly lower than reported by Stephen Wright for the period 1956 to 1984.[14] The mean turnout in runoffs for senators (compared with their first primaries)—of 89 percent—is slightly above the 87 percent figure for senators reported by Wright in his study covering twenty-eight years.

Relatively high voting rates in runoffs for state legislators (particularly state house members, who represented the smallest constituencies) support the personal contact hypothesis. However, the relatively high rate of participation in gubernatorial runoffs (more voter turnout in 34 percent of the cases, and an average turnout almost 92 percent as high as that of the initial primary) con-

Table 6.1 Comparison of Participation in Runoffs and
First Primaries, Controlling for Office, 1970–1986

Office	More Votes Cast in Runoff	Average Runoff Vote as a Percent of Primary Vote
Governorship	34.4%	91.7%
Lt. Governorship	30.8	89.1
Other statewide executive offices	9.7	85.1
U.S. Senate	20.8	89.4
U.S. House	16.1	79.6
State Senate	32.6	93.7
State House	38.1	95.8

forms with the visibility hypothesis. Lower voting rates for members of the
U.S. House and lesser statewide offices fit either the visibility or the personal
contact hypothesis.

State Portraits

In keeping with the personal contact thesis, the two states where declining
participation was the most prevalent (and where average runoff turnout was
lowest) were the ones for which we were unable to obtain data on state lower
house contests. Only one out of twenty runoffs in North Carolina, and one
out of thirty-nine in Texas, drew more voters than the first primary.[15] At the
other extreme, Alabama was the one state where runoffs generally attracted
more voters than the initial primary. In 63 percent of the Alabama runoffs,
more voters expressed preferences than in the initial primary. The only other
state where participation in a runoff often exceeded that in a first primary was
Georgia, where 47 percent of the time the runoff attracted more voters than
the first primary.

As a second measure of relative participation in the runoff, Table 6.2 reports average runoff voting as a share of primary votes cast. Alabama typi-

Table 6.2 Comparison of Participation in Runoffs
and First Primaries across States, 1970–1986

State	More Votes Cast in Runoff	Average Runoff Vote as a Percent of Primary Vote
Alabama	63.1%	103.0%
Arkansas	21.8	86.3
Florida	24.7	88.9
Georgia	46.5	100.8
Louisiana	27.6	89.9
Mississippi	25.8	97.7
North Carolina	5.0	77.2
Oklahoma	32.0	93.2
South Carolina	24.4	85.3
Texas	2.6	67.4

cally had more votes cast in the runoff, whereas in Georgia runoff turnout on average equaled participation in the first primary. Primary voters outnumbered runoff voters by the largest margins in North Carolina and Texas.[16] The decline in North Carolina is consistent with Lanier's observations for the Tarheel State during the period 1950–82.[17]

Election Cycles

Another piece of evidence that partially supports the proposition that local contests are more likely to stimulate participation comes from Table 6.3. The first column in the top row of the table shows the proportion of runoffs that had a higher vote tally than the corresponding first primary during off-year elections. In contention were statewide executive positions for seven states, along with most state legislative and county offices. In over 40 percent of the runoffs, more votes were cast in the runoff than in the primary; if 1986 is eliminated, the proportion of runoffs attracting more voters than the opening primaries rises to 48.4 percent.

Table 6.3 Comparison of Participation in Runoffs
and First Primaries over Time, 1970–1986

Cycle	More Votes Cast in Runoff	Average Runoff Vote as a Percent of Primary Vote
Off-year congressional (1970, 1974, 1978, 1982, 1986)	43.9%	97.5%
Presidential (1972, 1976, 1980, 1984)	23.5	87.6
Off-off year* (1971, 1975, 1979, 1983)	25.6	93.7

*Data are for Louisiana and Mississippi.

In the second row of Table 6.3 are figures for presidential-year primaries. In less than one-quarter of those cases were more votes cast in the runoff than in the primary. (Recall that, of the states examined, only in North Carolina are the most important statewide offices filled during presidential years.)

The anomaly in this table comes from the third row, which presents figures for Louisiana and Mississippi. As noted above, we have designated these contests off-off year elections because the election cycle for these states coincides with neither presidential nor congressional elections. The personal contact hypothesis suggests relatively higher turnout in off-off-year elections, as we observed for off-year runoffs. Contrary to expectations, the proportion of off-off-year runoffs attracting more voters is similar to that of the presidential-year contests, and average runoff voting in the off-off-year states is several percentage points below that in off years, although at 93.7 percent it is six points higher than for presidential years. The two measures, then, give different perspectives for off-off-year elections.

Turnout participation in the off-off-year states may be depressed by Louisiana's unique electoral system, whereby all candidates—Democrats, Republicans, and Independents—run in a single, open primary.[18] If no candidate polls a majority, the top two face off in a runoff, with most Louisiana runoffs featuring two Democrats.[19] The initial primary may have attracted large numbers of Republican voters who supported a Republican candidate, but these voters would have had little incentive to return to the polls a second time when their options were exclusively on the Democratic side. In keeping with this proposition, the average runoff vote as a share of the primary vote in Louisiana was 89.9 percent, eight points below that of Mississippi (see Table 6.2). But contrary to this reasoning, the share of runoffs that attracted more votes than the initial primaries was actually higher in Louisiana than in Mississippi (27.6 to 25.8 percent).

Party Differences

Looking next at the party variable, the evidence supports the expectation that Republican runoffs will attract fewer voters. As shown in Table 6.4, GOP voters participated in runoffs at higher rates than in the first primaries only one-eighth of the time. This compares with an increase in turnout for 36 percent of the Democratic elections.

Probably because it has fewer runoff contests, the Republican party does a poorer job of holding the commitment of its primary voters than does the Democratic party. Table 6.4 reports a twenty-percentage-point difference between the share of first-primary voters in the Democratic and Republican runoffs. This difference was particularly significant in U.S. House contests, where the participation ratio among Democrats was 90.5 percent compared with 61.8 percent for Republicans. Only for the positions of governor and lieutenant governor did the tallies in Republican runoffs exceed 80 percent of the votes cast in the first primary. A gubernatorial runoff is likely when GOP prospects for winning the chief executive post are good. The same expectations that drew multiple candidates into the Republican lists often inspired the GOP electorate to return to the polls for the decisive runoff. Among Democrats, the post of lieutenant governor and other lesser statewide positions were the only ones for which the vote ratio was less than 90 percent.

Patterns in Voter Participation over Time

A longitudinal review of the frequency with which runoffs drew more voters than primaries discloses two elements that may be useful for future research. In 82 percent of the runoffs across the South examined for 1970, more votes

Table 6.4 Comparison of Participation in Runoffs and
First Primaries, Controlling for Party, 1970–1986

Party	More Votes Cast in Runoff	Average Runoff Vote as a Percent of Primary Vote
Democratic	36.4%	95.6%
Republican	12.3	74.9

were cast in the second primary. But over three recent election years (1983–86), runoffs attracted more participation only 22 percent of the time.

Inspection of the full array of elections in our data set by year indicates that 1970 was unique: it was the only year in which participation in the runoff exceeded that in the primary. In 1976, 85 percent of the primaries attracted more voters than the runoffs, and that figure was nearly equaled in 1972 and 1975. In 1974, and for 1979 through 1982, approximately 55 percent of the primaries drew more voters than the runoffs. Thus, the results generally support the proposition that over time voter participation in runoffs has declined relative to the first primary. During the same period, Republican strength has gradually grown in the South, rebounding from the depths to which it plunged following Watergate and Jimmy Carter's 1976 sweep.

Competitiveness and First-Primary Strength

Two measures of competitiveness have been explored and neither discloses a strong relationship with runoff participation. First, the size of the margin between the first- and second-place finishers in the initial primary had a nonsignificant relationship with runoff voting as a proportion of the primary vote ($r = min.03$). And second, the Blacks' dichotomous measure of a primary leader's strength showed no relationship with whether more votes were cast in the runoff. Approximately 34 percent of the cases in both categories of the Blacks' measure attracted more voters in the second primary.

There is little evidence that runoff turnout was higher when the contenders had captured a larger share of the vote in the initial primary. The share of the total first-primary vote won by the participants in the runoff had only a weak relationship with runoff participation (r = .04).

Influence of Race on Turnout

Contests involving black candidates tended to stimulate greater participation than did all-white runoffs. In 55 percent of the runoffs with a black candidate, more voters registered preferences in the second primary. The comparable figure for increased voting in all-white runoffs was just one-third.

The greater participation in contests with black candidates could mean either that blacks and liberal whites mobilized to elect a black, or that conservative whites mobilized to defeat the black candidate. To explore which of these possibilities is more accurate, we examined the success of black runoff candidates by controlling statistically first for black winners, then for black losers. When a black candidate was nominated, more people had participated in the runoff than in the primary 44 percent of the time. In contrast, when a white defeated a black for the nomination, runoff participation rose in 64 percent of the contests. Average figures on runoff turnout indicate that 90 percent as many voters participated when blacks won nominations; when a white defeated a black, runoff voting averaged 103 percent of the primary vote.

Because we lack data on black and white turnout rates for primaries and runoffs, we risk making an incorrect inference. With that caveat in mind, we note that our findings are in line with the following interpretation: When the electorate turns out in greater numbers in the runoff, the black candidate is likely to lose. When the electorate is less enthusiastic about the runoff, the black candidate is likely to win nomination.

It remains for a later study to explore what stimulated higher turnout in runoffs where blacks were defeated. Did white candidates make racial appeals? Consider the one made by Sam Massell (a white), who, when opposing Maynard Jackson (a black) in a runoff for mayor of Atlanta, sought votes with the ominous message that Atlanta was "too young to die." Or did the black candidate have a rallying cry similar to that used by Chicago's Mayor Harold Washington, who boasted: "Our time has come?"[20] Efforts by either candidate to maximize the turnout of voters with whom he or she shares a racial tie may spark a countermobilization of the other race. Or did a sharp contrast in issue positions or the availability of two attractive and well-qualified candidates stir public enthusiasm? A more intensive look at runoffs involving a black and a white candidate is needed.

Influence of Gender on Turnout

Only weak evidence suggests that more voters go to the polls in runoffs involving female rather than all-male candidates. In our study, turnout increased one-third of the time in second primaries with a woman compared with 30 percent in all-male elections. In female-male runoffs, turnout was higher 37.5 percent of the time when a woman won, compared with higher turnout 30.5 percent of the time when a man won. Mean turnout figures were in the opposite direction, averaging 90 percent of primary participation when women won but 97 percent of the primary figure when women lost. Such inconsistencies hardly compel the conclusion that voters flock to the polls on election day either to deny nominations to women or to elect them.

Comparison with Other Research Findings

Wright's Study of Democratic Gubernatorial and Congressional Contests

The most extensive analysis of runoff turnout was conducted by Stephen Wright, who compared participation in Democratic gubernatorial and congressional primaries with their corresponding runoffs from 1956 to 1984.[21] Wright found that in 23 percent of his election pairs, runoffs attracted more voters than did the primaries. Wright's research covers seven election years before ours but stops one year before our study ends and omits state offices other than the governorship. Despite these dissimilar data sets, the general pattern of results is comparable. Perhaps because Wright's data cover an earlier period than ours, he has a slightly larger share of contests in which runoff participation exceeded first-primary participation in contests for governor and the U.S. House. Wright reports, however, that in only 10 percent of the senatorial contests did more voters cast their ballots in the runoff than in the first primary—half the rate we observed.

As one would expect, participation in U.S. House runoffs is more likely to decline in the absence of a statewide contest. Thus, Wright reports that runoff participation exceeded primary participation 25 percent of the time when the congressional runoff was coupled with a runoff for governor or the U.S. Senate, compared to a heightened runoff participation less than 19 percent of the time when the congressional election failed to coincide with a statewide runoff.

Bullock's Study of Urban Runoffs

A second work comparing primary and runoff turnout looked at thirty-seven sets of elections for six cities. The cities were ones for which Charles Bullock had primary and runoff data for at least a decade.[22] To ensure that the potential electorate was identical for both the runoff and the primary, Bullock considered only election pairs where both had at least one citywide contest. Overall, runoff voting was greater than primary voting in twenty-two elections (59.5 percent). In twenty of the runoffs, the turnout exceeded primary turnout by more than 5 percent, while in ten runoffs the decline from the primary exceeded 5 percent.

The general trend was for more voters to go to the polls in the runoff. Table 6.5 shows that in five out of six elections held in Tallahassee, runoff turnout was at least five percentage points higher than first-primary turnout. Runoffs also generally attracted more voters in Sarasota. Austin was the only city where primary turnout tended to exceed runoff turnout.

The findings of Wright and Bullock generally support our proposition that enthusiasm for local contests tends to produce runoffs that attract relatively large numbers of voters. The higher-level offices analyzed by Wright tended to have fewer voters in the runoff, whereas the municipal offices analyzed by Bullock generally had greater turnout in the runoff. Although we live in a media age that emphasizes the importance of television in

Table 6.5 Comparison of Primary and Runoff Turnout
in Selected Municipal Elections

City	Turnout in Runoffs Was		
	< 95% of First Primary	+ 5% of First Primary	> 5% above First Primary
Atlanta, Ga.	2	1	3
Austin, Tex.	2	1	1
Jackson, Tenn.	0	2	1
Pomona, Calif.	3	1	5
Sarasota, Fla.	2	2	5
Tallahassee, Fla.	1	0	5
Total	10	7	20
	27%	19%	54%

Source: Charles S. Bullock III, "Turnout in Municipal Elections," *Policy Studies Review* 9 (Spring 1990): 545.

politics, local personalized interest in candidates can still be a significant stimulus for voter participation.[23]

Bullock and Smith's Study of Georgia Counties

Further evidence on interelection (that is, primary versus runoff) participation comes from data on some four hundred elections in Georgia counties with sizable black populations, compiled by Charles Bullock and Brock Smith. (For more discussion of this data set, see chapter 4, "Black and White Runoffs for County Offices.") These were local elections; therefore, if the personal contact thesis explains runoff participation, we should find less dropoff in these elections than in those analyzed in Tables 6.1 through 6.4. Because offices were elected countywide or from districts within counties, sometimes the offices represented smaller constituencies than those examined in Bullock's study of urban elections (although that was not always the case). Support for the visibility hypothesis would find a greater drop-off in voter participation in runoffs for these county offices than for those in the main data set analyzed in this book.

The results for Georgia counties are in line with the personal contact thesis, however. The numbers of runoffs with increased and decreased participation rates were approximately equal, with declines occurring 52 percent of the time. Declining participation was less common than for the offices listed in Table 6.1 but more common than for the set of citywide elections presented in Table 6.5.

As shown in Table 6.6, of the county office races that more frequently went to runoffs, turnout tended to be higher in the runoff than in the first primary when the nomination of a sheriff was at stake (59 percent). Just the opposite pattern emerged in board of education contests, where primary voting exceeded runoff voting 60 percent of the time. In contests for county commissioner (which composed about half of the entire data set), there were approximately equal numbers of elections in which runoff voting increased or decreased.

The figures on average runoff participation are consistent with those regarding the frequency with which runoffs attracted more voters than the primary. On average, more voters participated in the runoff, than in the first primary, for sheriff. Table 6.6 further shows that the average runoff participation in county commissioner contests was slightly less than voting in the first primary, whereas participation lagged substantially in board of education runoffs. The figures for sheriff and commissioner are higher than those for any office in Table 6.1.

Traditionally, the sheriff has been the most powerful official in southern counties, so it is not surprising that a runoff to determine who will receive the nomination for that post has a way of attracting voters. The issues dealt with by county commissions are more encompassing than the school policies promulgated by boards of education, which may account for the difference in turnout patterns to elect the respective members of these collegial bodies.

Patterns in Voter Participation over Time

A longitudinal pattern is noticeable in these results, with runoff participation exceeding primary participation in at least three-fourths of the contests held

Table 6.6 Comparison of Participation in Runoffs and First Primaries for Selected Offices in Georgia Counties with Sizable Black Populations

Office	More Votes Cast in Runoff	Average Runoff Vote as a Percent of Primary Vote	N
Sheriff	59.1%	101.5%	41
Commissioner	50.9	97.6	204
Member, Board of Education	40.0	85.8	55

in 1970, 1974, and 1982. The figures on average runoff participation support the data on the frequency of increases in runoff voting in off-year elections reported in Table 6.3. In 1974 runoffs drew an average of 115.5 percent as many voters as did the first primary, and in 1982 the figure was 102.7 percent. The figure for 1970, while below 100 percent, was still high (97.7 percent). The element in common for these years was the presence of a gubernatorial runoff. In no other year was the nomination of the state's chief executive officer decided in a second primary. The drawing power of a gubernatorial primary supports the visibility hypothesis. The eagerness of Georgians to participate in the nomination of their next governor may explain why this state had relatively greater runoff participation than most other states (see Table 6.2).

It is likely that two factors were operating here. First, the need for a statewide runoff to nominate the chief executive officer may have encouraged some people to vote in the runoff who might otherwise have stayed away, and, second, other voters may have been drawn by contests to elect significant local officials, particularly the sheriff. Figures for 1978 allow comparison of a year in which there was no gubernatorial runoff but the same set of state and local officers were on the ballot. In that year, runoffs attracted an average of 89.8 percent as many voters as the first primary, and only one-third of the runoffs had more voters than the first primary. This underscores the drawing power of a gubernatorial runoff.

Statewide figures further point up this drawing power. In 1970, 54,000 more votes were tallied in the Democratic gubernatorial runoff than in the first primary; four years later, the gubernatorial runoff drew an additional 66,000 voters. In the 1982 gubernatorial runoff, 11,000 more votes were cast than in the first primary.[24]

Even a senatorial primary was unable to produce more runoff than first-primary voters. In 1980 scandal-haunted and hard-pressed four-term Democratic incumbent, Senator Herman Talmadge, was renominated in the runoff (in which 46,000 fewer ballots were tallied than in the first primary). The 1972 runoff, in which Democrat Sam Nunn (then a state legislator) defeated an interim appointee for the Senate, had almost 100,000 fewer voters than the first primary.

Influence of Race and Gender

Neither a black nor a woman on the ballot in a local Georgia runoff stampeded voters to the polls. When there was a black candidate in the race, the proportion of runoffs where more votes were cast than in the first primary was almost identical with the overall figures for the data set (although, on average, runoff voting was 3.5 percentage points higher when a black ran). When a woman competed in a runoff, voters were less likely to turn out, with only 40 percent of the runoffs that involved a woman attracting more voters than the first primary. The average number of votes cast when a woman ran was lower than in all-male runoffs.

When blacks won first primaries, turnout was as likely to have increased in the runoff as to have declined. When blacks lost runoffs, there was a slight tendency for voting to increase in the second primary (53 percent of the time). Among women, the frequency with which participation was greater in the runoff than the first primary was virtually identical when women both won and lost the nomination. Thus, we find no evidence to support the notion that racists or sexists typically turn out in excessive numbers to maintain white male control of an office (although this may happen in some instances). Or, one could argue, our approach fails to uncover whether racists or sexists vote in excessive numbers because women and blacks are more likely to stay away from the polls when one of their own is in a primary. This strikes us as an unlikely proposition.

Competitiveness and First-Primary Strength

The county-level data, like that for state and federal offices, provides little support for the proposition that more competitive initial primaries will be followed by runoffs where voting exceeds first-primary participation. The results using the 40-plus-5 dichotomous measure of front-runner strength in the first primary is not in the expected direction. Participation *rose* in 47.6 percent of the elections following a strong performance by the front-runner, compared with 44.3 percent of the contests in which the first primary was more competitive. The correlation between the runoff vote as a share of the primary vote and the size of the primary plurality is also contrary to the expected direction (r = -.09) and comes close to being significant at the .05 level. Thus, for both county-level and higher offices, we must reject the hypothesis that first-primary competitiveness is followed by greater participation in the runoff. Indeed, the weak patterns that are visible suggest precisely the opposite.

The share of the first-primary vote cast for the candidates who advanced to the runoff also fails to be related to runoff participation. We found a nonsignificant relationship between the share of the vote captured by the top two finishers in the first primary and relative runoff participation (r = .05).

Multivariate Analysis of Runoff Turnout

Multivariate analysis was used to determine which of the various factors considered for the 1,222-case data set are most important in helping us understand the extent to which runoff turnout approximated participation in the initial primary. The models tested in this chapter (below) contain variables that give signs of potential usefulness, based on the bivariate analyses presented above. In addition, we have retained some variables (such as sex and race), even though the bivariate analyses do not give a strong indication that these will be statistically important predictors.

The first column in Table 6.7 provides results from a logit analysis in which the dependent variable is whether the turnout in the runoff exceeded the vote in the initial primary. The second column presents regression coefficients for

Table 6.7 Multivariate Analyses of Runoff Turnout
(Standard Errors in Parentheses)

Variable	More Votes Cast in Runoff	Runoff Vote as a Percent of Primary Vote
Intercept	−2.805	.708
Party	−1.279 (.288)	−.187 (.035)
Share of primary vote for top 2 candidates	1.683 (.585)	.218 (.091)
State legislature	.592 (.204)	.059 (.030)
Off-year elections	.685 (.145)	.069 (.023)
Black in runoff	.801 (.335)	.020 (.056)
Woman in runoff	.247 (.192)	.025 (.031)
Alabama	1.038 (.204)	.060 (.035)
Georgia	.627 (.172)	.071 (.029)
Texas	−2.250 (1.029)	−.168 (.062)
Primary leader's margin	−1.598 (1.013)	−.097 (.159)

$R^2 = .07$

Adjusted $R^2 = .06$

Model chi square = 183.76

Correctly predicted = 72.8%

a model in which the dependent variable is the runoff vote as a percentage of the first-primary vote. The table lends support for the importance of a number of variables that showed promise in the bivariate analyses. For both the regression and logit analyses, runoff participation is depressed for Republican runoffs and for runoffs in Texas. The regression analysis indicates that Republican runoff participation was nineteen percentage points below the Democratic rate, all other things being equal. Runoff participation was higher in off-year elections than in other years, in Georgia and, to a lesser degree, Alabama, as well as in state legislative contests. Each of these items adds six or seven percentage points to runoff participation.

Another variable that is a statistically significant predictor is the share of the total primary vote polled by the two candidates who met in the runoff: the larger the share of the vote captured by these two candidates, the greater the participation in the runoff.

Biracial elections are more likely to have more votes cast in the runoff than in the first primary, but this variable was a weak predictor in the regression model (although it was significant in the logit model). Contests that included men and women were not more likely to attract runoff participation. Nor was the competitiveness in the initial primary (that is, the size of the primary leader's margin) associated with turnout in the runoff.

Although we have identified a number of predictors that are statistically significant, the overall effect of the models examined leaves much to be desired. The great bulk of the variance in the runoff vote as a percentage of primary turnout is not explained. Moreover, we had hoped that a larger share of the cases could be correctly classified with the logit model.

As noted earlier, in some contests the nominee attracts fewer votes than the plurality leader received in the first primary. The data sets for both state and federal offices, as well as for positions at the county level, show that only infrequently did the nominee get fewer votes than the primary leader. In approximately one-sixth of the state and federal contests, the vote for the primary leader exceeded that for the runoff winner. Figures for the county-level contests are almost identical, with the primary leader getting more votes than the runoff leader only 15 percent of the time. The nominee, then, usually received more votes than the primary leader, even if in approximately two-thirds of the state and federal contests the overall turnout in the runoff dropped below that in the initial primary.

Two Perspectives on Runoff Voting Frequency

Two broad perspectives have been explored to account for differences in the degree of first- and second-primary voting: the visibility hypothesis and the personal contact hypothesis. Some support has been found for each. The presence of a gubernatorial runoff seemed to draw additional voters to the polls in Georgia, which is in keeping with the visibility hypothesis. Runoffs for the U.S. Senate, however, lacked the drawing power of a gubernatorial contest, even though senators, like governors, share high visibility.

Overall, we have found more support for the personal contact hypothesis, with lower-level elections more likely to experience an increase in runoff voting than top-of-the-ticket elections. In addition, although a runoff typically attracted fewer voters than did the first primary, the nominee almost always polled more votes than the plurality leader was able to obtain in the first primary.

In the next—and concluding—chapter, we extend our analysis to the relationship between runoffs and general elections. Do runoff victors go on to win the contest that counts the most? We close with some thoughts about the future of the runoff in American elections.

7 An Appraisal of the Runoff

Runoffs were incorporated into the electoral landscape of the South at a time when two-party competition was rare. Many southern states adopted the majority-vote requirement during the first part of the century—after both Republicans and Populists had ceased to be a serious threat in statewide contests and were infrequently successful even in state legislative elections. States that made runoffs mandatory later, like Alabama and Arkansas, did so when Republican candidates were generally little more than a nuisance factor.

Given the historical intent of the runoff as a means to ensure majority support in the Democratic party and the fact that today's primaries are frequently multifactional, intraparty contests, some have suggested that the provision has outlived its usefulness. In other words, now that Republicans at least occasionally win statewide contests in every southern state, in addition to regularly winning the region's presidential votes, the runoff is unnecessary to ensure majority support for officeholders. William Keech and Carol Swain, for example, argue that "the runoff is now superfluous for its original purpose."[1]

Some observers have gone further, warning that the runoff actually harms the Democratic party. By prolonging the nomination phase of an election, the majority-vote rule may allow the animosities of feuding factions within the party to grow for an extended period.[2] After the first primary eliminates all but the two strongest competitors, supporters of the remaining candidates may become increasingly hostile. Sometimes these rivalries are so bitter that the loser's troops refuse to rally behind the runoff winner. Traditionally, there was no need to reunite the party as the runoff determined who would hold office. Leaders of feuding factions would often keep their weapons ready for the next election two or four years away. Putting aside differences and joining with recent foes to face a GOP challenger are responses many Democrats have yet to learn. The elongated primary season may hurt the Democratic party as it goes to the general election because, even if the loser supports the winner, there will be less time and perhaps fewer resources available for the general election campaign. The end result is, arguably, the nomination of a weakened Democrat who limps into battle against a well-rested Republican.

These worst-case scenarios actually came to pass in 1986. In Alabama, the winner of the Democratic gubernatorial runoff found himself challenged in court by supporters of the losing candidate. Attorneys for Lieutenant Governor Bill Baxley contended that Charlie Graddick won the runoff only because he received the votes of a number of Republicans who, in violation of state law, were allowed to vote in the second Democratic primary. According to Baxley, Graddick, who as attorney general was responsible for enforcing state statutes prohibiting voters from participating in a runoff if they had already cast ballots in the opposing party's primary that year, had invited GOP infiltration. Graddick anticipated Republican support, as he was the more conservative candidate in the runoff and had previously been a Republican.[3]

When a federal judge overturned the results of the ballot box, the Democratic party replaced Graddick with Baxley as the nominee. Graddick supporters festooned their cars with bumper stickers reading, "I'm Mad As Hell, Too, Charlie!" When Graddick called off a write-in campaign and endorsed the Republican, Alabama elected its first Republican governor in this century.

Another nightmare for the Democrats materialized in Florida. This state holds its primary and runoff later than other southern states. By the time a runoff is settled, there is only about a month until the general election. In 1986 the heated campaign for governor on the Democratic side required a runoff. This allowed little time for the runoff winner to construct a successful campaign against his GOP opponent. The winner of the Democratic runoff was dealt an additional blow when his runoff rival endorsed Republican Bob Martinez, who became the Sunshine State's second Republican chief executive.

Despite the suggestion that in such instances the runoff may have jeopardized Democratic hopes in November, many Democrats continue to support the majority-vote requirement. Among its boosters is Andrew Young, formerly a congressman, mayor of Atlanta, and ambassador to the United Nations. Young opposed a suit brought by several other black politicians in 1990 challenging the Georgia majority-vote rule. He explained his support for the runoff this way: "Well, I think when you carry a majority of the Democratic party, you, first of all, have a better chance of winning the general election, and then once winning the general election, you have a demonstrated majority support to enable you to govern. . . . around the world, minority governments are not functioning well." [4]

Young had reason to support the majority-vote requirement, as he finished second in his initial bid to become mayor of Atlanta. It was only by winning a runoff that he became the city's chief executive. Shortly after making the above statement, Young placed second in Georgia's Democratic gubernatorial primary. In this contest, however, he failed in the runoff to overcome his initial second-place finish.

Andrew Young is not alone in believing that the runoff often advantages Democratic nominees. Merle and Earl Black observed that "in the absence of a strong statewide party organization capable of selecting and promoting attractive candidates for the general election, the dual primary strengthens the electoral chance of Democratic nominees in general elections by providing a mechanism for eliminating many weak frontrunners." [5]

This chapter explores two issues that must enter into any appraisal of the runoff's future. First, how widespread is Republican opposition in the general election? If Republicans are generally mounting serious campaigns, then the need for a runoff to ensure that officeholders maintain majority support may no longer exist. (The runoff might still be useful, however, to ensure that a party will nominate a mainstream candidate rather than allowing the candidate of a splinter group to win nomination with a plurality.) And second, what is the fate of candidates who survive runoffs? Are they especially susceptible to defeat in November? Are nominations won through runoffs merely Pyrrhic victories?

The elections analyzed in this chapter include all contests for the U.S. Congress and for governor. Also covered are legislative contests in the states for which we obtained general election results to complement runoff returns: Alabama, Florida, Georgia, Mississippi, and Oklahoma.

Frequency of Interparty Competition

In over 40 percent of the elections surveyed, the Democratic nominee faced no Republican opponent in the general election. Despite growth in Republican strength in the South, the frequency of unopposed Democratic victories following a runoff has remained fairly steady. In 1970, 37.8 percent of the Democratic runoff winners had no opposition in November, a figure identical with that for 1984 and similar to that for 1986 (33.8 percent). As recently as 1982, 47.7 percent of the Democrats nominated in runoffs faced no further obstacle to taking office. The absence of Republicans was particularly pronounced in Alabama and Georgia, where 52.8 and 60.9 percent (respectively) of the runoff winners had no Republican opponent.

The absence of opposition from the GOP is concentrated in state legislative contests. Republican opposition confronted every Democrat who won a runoff for a seat in the U.S. Senate or to become governor, and all but one U.S. House winner faced a Republican opponent (see Table 7.1). Among Democratic state legislators, however, more than half were unopposed in the general election. On the Republican side, Democratic opposition was more common, even for a seat in the legislature. Only one in fifteen Republican winners in state legislative races escaped a Democratic challenge.

The likelihood of a Democrat meeting a Republican in the general election is linked to the degree of factionalism that takes place in the first primary. Almost half of the Democratic runoff winners who competed in the initial primary with three candidates were unopposed by the GOP in November. Runoff winners who emerged from four- or five-person fields were unopposed in November just over 40 percent of the time. When candidates won runoffs after competing against six or more candidates in the first primary, they faced Republican opposition more than 90 percent of the time. Perhaps large fields of Democrats, which may indicate extreme factionalism, lead Republicans to believe that their chances are enhanced by the pronounced internecine struggle within the Democratic party and the fluid situation that accompanies the political uncertainty of multiple candidacies.

The notion that runoffs are no longer necessary, as bipartisan competition will ensure that officeholders receive majority support, appears to be inaccu-

Table 7.1 General Election Outcomes for Democrats
Nominated in Runoff, by Office, 1970–1986

Office	Democrat Defeated Republican	Democrat Lost to Republican	Democrat Was Unopposed	N
Governorship	76.9	23.1	0	26
Other statewide office	72.7	0	27.3	11
U.S. Senate	44.4	55.6	0	18
U.S. House	57.7	41.2	1.2	85
State Senate	46.5	4.4	49.1	114
State House	39.0	8.6	52.4	454
Total	44.5	13.4	42.1	708

rate. As we discovered when evaluating the leader-loses and incumbent-loses myths (chapter 2), experiences at the top of the ticket should not be broadly generalized. Winners of statewide nominations and candidates for the U.S. House usually survive a general election. At least half of the Democratic contenders for state legislative positions—and most state legislators in the South continue to be Democrats—assumed office without opposition in the general election.

Although our data do not include elections for local office, we suspect that bipartisan competition is less frequent at this level than for state legislators. The rural South continues to be steadfastly Democratic, while a growing number of suburban counties have become solidly Republican. Thus, most local officeholders may escape partisan opposition altogether.

The Impact of Runoffs on General Elections

More than three-quarters of the Democrats who were nominated in a runoff and faced a Republican won the general election. The comparable figure for

Republicans who faced Democratic opposition was only 56 percent. In both parties, runoff winners who emerged from more competitive initial primaries were more likely to overcome opposition in the general election than were nominees who experienced less competition in the first primary. Here we divide the data (see Table 7.2), using the Blacks' 40-plus-5 rule—that is, noncompetitive primaries are those where the front-runner received at least 40 percent of the vote and led the second-place finisher by at least five percentage points.

Evidence that candidates who emerged from more competitive initial primaries performed better in contested general elections runs counter to the expectation that a heated contest will weaken the nominee. The interpretation for Table 7.2 suggests that to a degree—and particularly among Republicans—less competition in the primary foreshadows likely defeat in the general election. That could help explain why Republican nominees from noncompetitive initial primaries did so much worse in general elections: they faced less of a challenge in the first primary perhaps because the nomination was seen as less likely to result in a general election victory. When the odds of actually winning the office are greater, first primaries more often attract at least two viable competitors so that no one compiles a sizable lead. Thus, as the prospect of winning the office increases so does the likelihood of a competitive primary—at least for Democrats.

A second test of the proposition that competitiveness for the nomination is associated with defeat in the general election focuses on the division of the runoff vote. As Table 7.3 reveals, Democrats chosen in competitive runoffs (that is, they won less than 55 percent of the vote) had a slight tendency to lose general elections more often than Democrats who got at least 55 percent of the vote in the runoff. Among Republicans, the difference between the two groups was even smaller: nominees in competitive runoffs tended to win more often than nominees who got at least 55 percent of the vote in the first primary. For neither party, however, were the disparities great, so that competitive runoffs do not appear to have endangered the winner.

Once again, a fuller compilation of election results shows that neither competitive runoffs nor first primaries consistently weakened nominees as they entered general elections. For the widespread but inaccurate generalization, the

Table 7.2 General Election Outcomes, Controlling for
Competitiveness of First Primary, 1970–1986

	Rate at Which Nominee Won General Election			
	Democrats		Republicans	
	%	N	%	N
Primary competitive	80.6	247	68.2	44
Primary noncompetitive	71.2	163	46.4	56

Note: Cases where the runoff nominee faced no opposition in the general election
have been eliminated.

Table 7.3 General Election Outcomes, Controlling for
Competitiveness of Runoff, 1970–1986

	Rate at Which Nominee Won General Election			
	Democrats		Republicans	
	%	N	%	N
Runoff competitive	74.9	207	57.5	40
Runoff noncompetitive	78.8	203	55.0	60

Note: Cases where the runoff nominee faced no opposition in the general election
have been eliminated.

culprit was a familiar one—top-of-the-ticket contests. Recall from Table 7.1
that Democratic congressional nominees stumbled almost half the time in November, while gubernatorial nominees lost almost a quarter of their elections.

Based on their study of gubernatorial campaigns, Earl and Merle Black
have speculated that the runoff strengthens a party when it eliminates an aging
former officeholder in favor of new blood.[6] The Blacks explain that the name
recognition of a longtime political figure may be sufficient for that person to
lead the initial field. But this individual may not be the strongest candidate
for the general election, and the runoff permits a hard-charging new face to
win the nomination.

We did not collect information on previous officeholding experience, other than to note whether an incumbent was in the runoff. Incumbents who successfully defended themselves in the runoff were particularly potent in the general election. In 95 percent of the forty runoffs in which an incumbent Democrat was renominated, that individual won reelection. When an incumbent was eliminated by a challenger in the runoff, the new standard bearer won election 84 percent of the time. Thus, we did not find that a party is strengthened when new blood wins the runoff. The least successful nominees were those who won a runoff for an open seat. These nominees won elections against Republicans only 73 percent of the time, perhaps because they lacked the name recognition and failed to attract the extensive media coverage that usually accompanies campaigns featuring well-known incumbents.

We found some modest indication that complacency may lead to the defeat of Democratic runoff victors. Three-quarters of the Democrats who led both primaries defeated Republicans, compared with 80 percent of the Democratic nominees who overcame a second-place finish in the initial primary. Perhaps the drive that allowed these second-place finishers to come from behind in the runoff made them stronger candidates in the general election.

Several Democratic politicians have worried that if a change from a majority-vote rule to a plurality rule resulted in the nomination of greater numbers of blacks, the ultimate beneficiary would be the Republican party. The logic is that if white Democrats will not vote for a black in the runoff, neither will they support a black nominee against a white Republican.

Our assessment of this theory is handicapped by the limited number of black nominees who confronted Republican opposition at this level of office seeking (U.S. Congress, governorship, state legislature). Three out of four blacks who defeated a white in a runoff lost in the general election. This contrasts with only two out of nine whites who defeated a black in the runoff and then succumbed to a Republican in November. (Instances where there was no Republican opposition have been excluded from this assessment of general election results. When the runoff was between two blacks, there was no Republican candidate in ten of the twelve cases, and in the other two instances, the black nominee won office.)

In their study of runoffs at the county level in Georgia, Charles Bullock and Brock Smith did not find that black nominees were susceptible to Republicans, as Republicans rarely entered the local contests.[7] Neither the Bullock and Smith data nor the data used in this study are sufficient to test the hypothesis that black nominees will be more vulnerable than white nominees in general elections. In both studies, black nomineess often were unopposed in the general election.

In discussing the potential impact of a 40 percent threshold, we warned that a structural change may stimulate behavioral changes. A similar caveat is appropriate here. If black nominees become more numerous in racially mixed constituencies, Republicans may less often allow general elections to go uncontested in these jurisdictions. Should that occur, our few cases hint that a white Republican might often defeat a black Democrat. More evidence, however, is needed to reach even a tentative conclusion.

Multivariate Analysis of Primary Competitiveness

Although the bivariate analyses of primary competitiveness reported in Table 7.2 and 7.3 indicate that a stiff challenge does not harm the nominee, a more convincing test requires a multivariate analysis. In the model we assign two variables indicating whether the first primary and the runoff were competitive. As control variables we include the office, the number of candidates in the initial primary, and the incumbency status and gender of the Democratic nominee. The office variable (where contests for Congress or the governorship are coded 1 and other offices are coded 0) is used because of the frequency with which we have observed that top-of-the-ticket experiences differ from those of other positions. The size of the primary field, we suspect, indicates, among other things, the expected probability of success in the general election. More people will enter the Democratic primary when Democrats are likely to win. Women may face opposition from less enlightened voters, thus damaging their general election prospects. Although an incumbent who has been forced into a runoff obviously has some political warts, our bivariate analyses indicate that the weaknesses that necessitated a runoff do not spill over into the general election.

The multivariate analysis, which appears in Table 7.4, shows that competi-

Table 7.4 Multivariate Model for Democratic Success
in General Elections after a Runoff, 1970–1986

Variable	Coefficient	Standard Error	Chi Square
Intercept	.887		
Runoff strength	.315	.258	1.49
Primary strength	−.346	.269	1.66
Office	−1.565	.290	29.04
Number of primary candidates	.191	.084	5.21
Incumbent	1.049	.390	7.21
Gender	−.636	.333	3.64

Model chi square = 49.83

Correctly predicted = 76.8%

N = 413

tiveness in neither the runoff nor the primary made Democratic nominees more susceptible in the general election. These results were expected from the bivariate analyses. The office being contested was a strong correlate of general election success, with success being less common for candidates seeking a congressional seat or the governorship. The finding of an office effect further underlines the difference between top-of-the-ticket and other contests. Democratic nominees were more likely to be elected when there was a large field of primary candidates and when the nominee was an incumbent. They were also somewhat more likely to be elected if they were male.

Evidence that competitiveness in the primary and the runoff has little effect on the outcome of general elections parallels findings reported by Steven Haeberle.[8] He sought to explain the variance in the share of the vote won by Democratic candidates for governor and senator who competed between 1932 and 1986. Although his model accounts for 55 percent of the variance, variables for the presence of Democratic and Republican runoffs are statistically insignificant.

We did not test the possibility that nominees who win without a runoff, or who face no primary opposition, succeed more often than do nominees chosen in a runoff. What we have demonstrated is that the competitiveness of the selection process among candidates in a runoff is not an important factor in who wins the general election.

So far in this chapter we have explored two suggested consequences of runoffs and have found support for neither. There are still numerous instances where Republicans do not field a candidate and, consequently—below the congressional level—it appears that the runoff is still necessary to ensure that officeholders obtain a majority of the vote. Moreover, we have found no support for the proposition that Democratic runoffs promote the election of a Republican. Even in the wake of a competitive runoff, three-fourths of the Democratic nominees who faced Republicans were elected. Incumbents who won renomination in a second primary almost always prevailed in the general election, despite the evidence that they had problems because they were forced into a runoff.

These results help us place the effects of the runoff into a broader context. Our final task in this volume is to offer an overall appraisal of the dual-primary system.

Sizing Up the Runoff

In 1988, shortly before challenges to the legality of runoff elections in Georgia and Memphis, Tennessee, a new state—Arizona—entered the ranks of those states endorsing the majority-vote procedure. Evidently, the rationale that prompted adoption of the runoff in the South is compelling to other electorates, too. The desire to be governed by officials chosen by a *majority* of the electorate remains strong among many voters in this nation.

When several black state legislators challenged the majority-vote requirement in Georgia, two blacks who were running strong races for statewide offices dissociated themselves from the suit. Andrew Young, who was seeking the Democratic nomination for governor at the time, said: "I'm not interested in only winning the Democratic primary. I'm interested in being governor." [9] Young believed that a nomination won with a plurality would be less likely to withstand a Republican challenge in the general election than would a nomination conferred by a majority of the Democratic electorate.

State senator Al Scott, a candidate for the Georgia Public Service Commission, also saw no advantage accruing from a change to a plurality rule. Indeed, Scott characterized such a step as likely to "create chaos, confusion and possibly a [white voter] backlash," adding: "I don't want to change the rule for this election." [10]

The concerns of Young and Scott echo statements made by various white political leaders in the South. Some have warned that if plurality nominations produced candidates who were unacceptable to most Democrats, then the elimination of the majority-vote requirement might be the biggest boon for the GOP since its resurgence began in 1964 with the presidential candidacy of Barry Goldwater.

A second reason for retaining the majority-vote requirement is the antithesis of the partisan concern expressed by Democrats. In much of the South, viable two-party competition is virtually nonexistent. In central cities and in many ruralcommunities, Republicans rarely field candidates. In a growing number of suburban counties, the Republican hammerlock is just as tight as that enjoyed by Democrats elsewhere. The farther down the pecking order of public offices one goes, the more likely that two-party competition will be absent. Table 1.2 in chapter 1 gives a hint of this but just at the congressional and gubernatorial levels. In state legislative elections, the frequency with which only one party fields a candidate increases. The figures rise yet again when local posts are included. In much of the South, therefore, the initial rationale for runoffs persists.

Nonpartisan cities provide an electoral environment analogous to the one-party South. Not surprisingly, many cities—most of which are nonpartisan—require that officeholders be endorsed by a majority of those voters expressing preferences. The avoidance of splinter candidates for public office is an objective widely pursued.

Are Runoffs Spreading?

Following the election of Evan Mecham as governor of Arizona in 1986, with 40 percent of the vote (an Independent candidate siphoned off 26 percent), state legislators passed a law requiring a majority vote in the general election for the state's top five positions. Mecham's subsequent impeachment and removal from office contributed to the concern over the quality of officeholders produced by the plurality vote. In the first election after the enactment of this provision, a runoff proved necessary when both major party candidates finished with slightly over 49 percent of the ballots.[11]

Perhaps only the fact that it has so far avoided the national embarrassment of a Mecham-like candidate has kept Maine from adopting a majority vote. In 1974 the state elected an Independent as governor with 40 percent of the vote. Four years later he was replaced by a Democrat who polled 48 percent. Eight years later the Democrat was succeeded by a Republican who also failed to achieve a majority, receiving 40 percent of the vote against three other candidates. By 1989 some Democrats in the state legislature explored the possibility of mandating a majority-vote in the general election for governor. This legislation has yet to be adopted.

Kentucky, unlike Arizona or Maine, lacks spirited two-party competition or troubling candidacies by Independents and has a partisan environment more like that found to the south.[12] More than twenty years have passed since a Republican occupied the governor's mansion. With the Democratic nomination providing the keys to the governor's office (and to other leadership positions), competition in the Democratic primary has been heated—usually producing three serious contenders. In none of the four Democratic gubernatorial primaries between 1979 and 1991 was there a clear favorite. As Table 7.5 shows, none of the last four Kentucky governors won nomination with even as much as 38 percent of the vote; in 1979 John Y. Brown fell short of the 30 percent threshold. The failure to attain the 40 percent plurality standard recently adopted by North Carolina (see chapter 5) and New York City (see chapter 3) had clearly been a problem for these candidates and other serious contenders in previous years.

In Kentucky, the governorship is not the only office for which nominees frequently win with relatively small shares of the vote. Joining the Democratic gubernatorial nominee in 1987 with less than 40 percent of the vote were Democratic nominees for treasurer, superintendent of public instruction, secretary of state, and lieutenant governor, along with the Republican gubernatorial nominee. Indeed, none of these candidates garnered the 34.9 percent of the vote won by the Democratic gubernatorial nominee.

Table 7.5 Division of the Vote among Serious Democratic Gubernatorial
Primary Contenders in Kentucky, 1979–1991

Candidate	1979	1983	1987	1991
John Y. Brown	29.1%*		25.8%	
Harvey Sloane	24.7	33.3%		
Terry McBrayer	23.2			
Carroll Hubbard	12.1			
Thelma Stovall	8.4			
Martha Layne Collins		34.0*		
Grady Stumbo		30.3	13.4	
Wallace Wilkinson			34.9*	
Steve Beshear			18.1	
Julian Carroll			6.6	
Brereton Jones				37.6%*
Scotty Baesler				30.4
Dr. Floyd G. Poore				26.8
Gatewood Galbraith				5.2

*Nominated and elected governor.

In 1983 and 1979, five statewide candidates other than governor were
nominated with pluralities. Although Governor Julian Carroll drew almost
two-thirds of the vote when seeking renomination by the Democratic party in
1975, seven other Democrats were nominated to statewide posts that year with
less than a majority.

The 1991 primaries once again resulted in five out of eight statewide Democratic nominees obtaining less than 40 percent of the vote. The nominees for
treasurer and superintendent of education each advanced to the general election after lackluster showings in which they attracted less than a quarter of
the vote.

Plurality nominations proved contagious in 1991, when four Republican statewide nominations were won by pluralities. Across the two parties, ten nominations to state executive posts were sought by more than two candidates. Nine of the ten went to plurality winners. In 1975, 1979, 1983, and 1991, of those nominated with less than a majority, most got less than 40 percent of the vote. Martha Layne Collins, who in 1983 became the Democratic nominee for governor with 34 percent of the vote, made a career of plurality nominations. In 1979 she was nominated for the post of lieutenant governor with only 23.2 percent of the vote; four years earlier she became her party's nominee for agriculture commissioner with just over a third of the ballot.

The small pluralities for Democratic nominees who went on to win elections in Kentucky is reminiscent of the situation that gave rise to adoption of the majority vote in Arkansas (see chapter 3). Kentucky has had some experience with runoffs, which are required for nonpartisan posts such as judgeships as well as for positions in many municipalities. Further, when the state initially switched from nominating through party conventions to a primary system, the election laws mandated a majority-vote provision. A runoff was held for governor in 1935 but was eliminated the next year.

In anticipation of the 1991 elections, reformers in the state senate introduced legislation to establish the majority-vote requirement in 1990. As it was initially proposed, a majority vote would have been necessary for nomination to any of the state's eight constitutional offices. But as the proposal wended its way through the legislature, the provision was watered down so as to apply only to contests for governor and lieutenant governor. Moreover, legislators substituted a 40 percent threshold in lieu of a majority vote.[13]

Arguments offered by supporters of the bill, which passed the senate, echoed those voiced in other states in other times. Said the sponsor: "I think you'll have a stronger candidate and a stronger person in office if they [*sic*] have a majority of the Democrats' support."[14] Perhaps in a reference to the incumbent governor, Wallace Wilkinson, whose campaign featured a pledge to use a state lottery rather than increase taxes, some runoff supporters noted that requiring a majority—or even 40 percent—would guard against the nomination of single-issue candidates.

Opponents of the runoff countered that a second campaign would increase election costs and that these added costs might disadvantage rural candidates. Some of Governor Wilkinson's supporters feared that if his wife sought to succeed him, she would be handicapped if a plurality were insufficient.[15] The only black senator in the state legislature voted against the bill, contending that it might disadvantage blacks—when and if an African American launched a serious statewide campaign.[16]

As noted previously, Republicans have generally supported challenges to the majority-vote requirement and Democrats have seen a majority vote as a safeguard for their party. Kentucky Republicans, though, had a far different outlook. One GOP senator explained his support of the runoff bill in these words: "After you folks bleed each other to death in two primary elections . . . we will be ready to pick up the pieces."[17]

Despite support by thirty-three out of thirty-seven voting senators, the Kentucky runoff bill died in the house. The house committee chair, a Democrat from Louisville, feared that candidates from his home county might be disadvantaged if they needed 40 percent or more of the vote for nomination. (Louisville's mayor, Jerry Abramson, was seen as a possible gubernatorial candidate.) An additional rationale for killing the bill seemed compelling to some opponents: Kentucky already had too many elections. The house speaker, who had initially pledged to work on behalf of the bill, changed his mind. Some observers attribute this reversal to his concern that the governor's allies might try to block an education bill dear to the speaker.

In the wake of the 1991 general election, when the Democratic gubernatorial nominee—along with nominees for several other constitutional offices who had attracted relatively small shares of the primary electorate—swept easily to victory, efforts to set a minimal threshold for the primary may be rekindled. The new governor, Brereton Jones, has voiced support for a majority-vote requirement, although he might wish to restrict its application to gubernatorial primaries.

The recent experiences of two other states may also have stimulated thoughts of electoral reform. In 1990 Alaska and Connecticut elected Independents as governors with less than half of the vote. Legislators in these states may believe that a switch to a majority-vote provision would advance party objectives. Indeed, fragmentation of the electorate in other constituencies across the nation may prompt a reevaluation of existing electoral standards, with an eye toward ensuring broad-based support for those who lead our governments.

The Future of the Runoff Primary

From time to time other electoral procedures, such as the approval voting technique, have been advanced to encourage majority outcomes in elections. However, the dual-primary system has an important advantage: it is easily understood by the average voter, who is apt to be skeptical of mathematically complicated methods designed to overcome Condorcet paradoxes and other arcane maladies that may afflict the best of democratic aspirations.

A first primary affords each candidate an opportunity to achieve a majority vote (or perhaps a 40 percent threshold vote) right at the beginning. If none is successful at this stage, the second primary—in terms simple and understandable—places the top two contenders against one another; the winner then comes away with a majority of the vote. Here is tangible, easily understood arithmetic: a majority of 50 percent plus one. At this point, the nominee of Party A faces the nominee of Party B in the general election (if Party B fields a candidate).

For those party officials seeking the legitimacy of majoritarianism without resorting to convoluted procedures that—however more virtuous they may be—might baffle and alienate voters, the runoff primary holds obvious appeal. Whether this dual system should be rejected on other grounds—say, that it discriminates against black or female candidates or that it is too costly—is another matter. In our research, we have found considerable evidence (presented throughout this book) that the runoff is far less biased than conventional wisdom would have it. To summarize our findings:

> Southerners turned to the runoff as a means for ensuring, in an essentially one-party region, that the Democratic nominee was the preference of a majority of the voters (although, for some, this rule may have had the purpose of protecting segregationist policies as well).

Almost 10 percent of the primaries for U.S. senator, U.S. representative, and governor led to a runoff, and in contested primaries a runoff was necessary in about one-fourth of the cases. Runoffs occurred most frequently for the governorship, as well as when no incumbent was in the race and when the contest took place within the Democratic party.

Contrary to conventional wisdom, the primary leader won the runoff about 70 percent of the time, although the success rate was lower for governors (56 percent) and U.S. senators (54 percent). Further, the wider the lead of the primary front-runners, the more apt they were to win the runoff. Also contrary to conventional wisdom, front-running incumbents went on to achieve renomination almost two-thirds of the time, and women who placed first in a primary were overwhelmingly likely to win nomination.

In cases of judicial intervention, the courts generally supported the constitutionality of the runoff provision.

In local contests, African American candidates were as likely to serve on city councils in majority-vote cities as in plurality cities. Black candidates also won more runoff elections at the county level than had formerly been the case (though black front-runners with weak first-primary leads performed less well than their white counterparts). Further, black candidates did less well in runoffs at statewide and federal levels of office seeking. A 40 percent threshold rule for runoffs (the North Carolina approach) may advantage black candidates and incumbents, although it is unclear what impact, if any, a change in electoral rules would have on candidate recruitment and voter behavior.

Voters were more likely to turn out for runoffs in local elections, perhaps because they knew the candidates personally. Although runoffs typically attracted fewer voters than the first primary, the nominee almost always polled more votes than the plurality front-runner was able to garner in the opening skirmish.

Democratic runoffs did not promote the election of Republicans. Even in the wake of a competitive second primary, fully three-fourths of the Democratic nominees who faced Republicans were elected.

Finally, incumbents who won renomination in a runoff almost always succeeded in the November election, despite the evidence of some weaknesses that had forced them into a second primary.

The data on the runoff remain imperfect—especially for black candidates in local elections, a difficult group to identify through archival research. It is ironic—in a nation that places great value on democracy—that it should be so difficult to obtain reliable information on elections. Thus, we end this book with a call for further efforts to gather and analyze data on the runoff and its effects. We hope that the findings presented here will stimulate ongoing interest and inquiry into what may well be America's least understood electoral procedure.

Notes

Preface

1. See Riker, *Liberalism against Populism*, pp. 74–77; Duncan Black, *The Theory of Committees and Elections*.
2. Letter to the *New York Times*, September 11, 1990, p. A18.
3. Merrill, *Making Multicandidate Elections More Democratic*. Prior to adopting the runoff, Alabama used a variant of approval voting in which voters indicated their first and second choices. If no candidate received a majority, the least popular candidate was eliminated and his or her votes were allocated to the voters' second preferences. This process of eliminating the relatively unpopular candidates and reallocating their votes continued until one candidate had a majority.

Chapter 1

1. See Lush, "Primary Elections and Majority Nominations," p. 43.
2. Alexander, "The Double Primary," p. 234.
3. Black, "A Theory of Southern Factionalism," p. 601.
4. See, generally, Ewing, *Primary Elections in the South*, pp. 4–7; Ladd, *American Political Parties*, pp. 137–39; Key, *Southern Politics*, pp. 416–23. For a claim that southerners adopted the runoff to help preserve the racial status quo, see Kousser, "Historical Origins," p. 8. Earl Black's analysis of southern gubernatorial primaries found that from 1945 to 1964 the runoff generally resulted in the nomination of the more outspoken advocate of segregation. In some contests a candidate who ran as a racial moderate swerved to the right in the runoff and charged his opponent with being soft on segregation. Since 1964, the black vote has become sufficiently large so that serious gubernatorial candidates have generally eschewed racial appeals (Black, *Southern Governors*).

5. See the sources in n. 4 above, as well as those listed in Table 1.1. The ten states examined in this study are Alabama, Arkansas, Florida, Georgia, Louisiana, Mississippi, North Carolina, Oklahoma, South Carolina, and Texas.

6. Park, "The Elusive Majority," p. 675.

7. Murphy, "Two Trials of Oklahoma's Runoff Primary," p. 157, n. 5.

8. Alexander, "The Double Primary," p. 225.

9. Letter from Brooks Hays to Alexander, May 11, 1944, in ibid., p. 226.

10. Ewing, *Primary Elections in the South*, p. 5.

11. Woodward, *Strange Career of Jim Crow*, p. 620.

12. Ladd, *American Political Parties*, pp. 138–39.

13. For GOP inroads into the South, see Black and Black, *Politics and Society in the South*, pp. 309–16. "As an institution, the Democratic primary is declining in importance," the authors write. "Though it is still used in most southern states to nominate candidates, such nominations are no longer equivalent to election" (pp. 178–79). See also Bullock, "Creeping Realignment in the South."

14. See, for example, Jesse Jackson, "Moving to the Common Ground"; Smeal, "Eleanor Smeal Report," p. 1.

15. Ewing, *Primary Elections in the South*. See also Canon, "Factionalism in the South."

16. Bullock and MacManus, "Municipal Electoral Structure"; Bullock and Smith, "Black Success in Local Runoff Elections."

17. In order to have a comparable data set with which to assess the topics of this chapter, we have eliminated state offices other than governor. Moreover, use of the electoral office contested by primary within each major party as the unit of analysis made impractical the task of extending this study down to state house and senate contests. The entire South has had approximately 110 members of Congress during the period studied. Because every state's legislature in the region has more than 110 seats, to include state legislative elections would have resulted in a data set many times the size of the current one.

18. The five standard bearers chosen from the ranks of current or recently retired governors since 1970 are Carter in 1976 and 1980, Reagan in 1980 and 1984, and Dukakis in 1988.

19. Schantz, "Contested and Uncontested Primaries," pp. 545–62.

20. Jacobson and Kernell, *Strategy and Choice*.

21. John R. Bond, "The Influence of Constituency Diversity."

22. Kuklinski, "Representativeness and Elections"; Elling, "Ideological Change"; Thomas, "Election Proximity."

23. Glenn R. Parker, "Members of Congress and Their Constituents," p. 181.

24. Haeberle, "Rundown on the Runoff."

25. Canon, "Factionalism in the South"; Wright, "The Number of Candidates"; Stanley, Bianco, and Niemi, "Partisanship and Group Support over Time."

26. Haeberle, "Rundown on the Runoff," p. 10, discerned no trend in gubernatorial and senatorial runoff frequency for 1932 to 1986.

27. A study of primary competition for southern congressional seats found that between 1956 and 1986, 408 of 1,164 Democratic incumbents were opposed and 115 had multiple challengers. Of 323 GOP incumbents, only 22 had a primary contest and of these, 4 featured multiple challengers. Thielemann, "Rise and Stall of Southern Republicans in Congress."

28. Schantz, "Contested and Uncontested Primaries."

29. Haeberle, "Rundown on the Runoff," p. 13.

30. A study of the House freshman class of 1970 found that incumbents tended to report *doing* better in the election than they had expected. Bullock, "Explaining Congressional Elections." It is likely that even the unbeatable will rarely ignore a challenger, thus the fears of GOP strategists are not groundless.

31. While it appears that contested primaries may be associated with susceptibility in the general election for Democratic nominees, Thielemann ("Rise and Stall of Southern Republicans in Congress") contends that Republican primary competition is associated with a stronger showing by the GOP nominee in the general election. Of course, it is possible that primary competitiveness among Republicans occurs when they perceive a high probability of winning the office, whereas among Democrats fierce competition may signal a weak incumbent or heir apparent. Competitive Republican primaries may help build the party by providing a reason for voters to request a GOP ballot. Southern Republican leaders like Haley Barbour see participation in a GOP primary as an important step in the partisan realignment of voters who regularly support Republican presidential nominees while continuing to think of themselves as Democrats.

Based on an analysis of gubernatorial runoffs, Black and Black argue that if the runoff eliminates a fading star in the Democratic party whose name recognition carried him to the front of the pack, it actually strengthens this party. Black and Black, "Democratic Gubernatorial Runoff Primaries."

Chapter 2

1. Baxter, "Second Place," p. A7.

2. Sherman, "Samples, 24, Tops Byron," p. B1.

3. Baxter, "Second Place," p. A7.

4. Caldwell, *The Caldwell Conspiracy*, pp. 75, 79; Foster quoted by Claybrook, telephone interview, March 5, 1992.

5. Sanders, telephone interview with Loch K. Johnson, 1984.

6. Alexander, "The Double Primary," p. 256.

7. Liebling, *The Earl of Louisiana*, pp. 85, 19.

8. Ewing, *Primary Elections in the South*, p. 88; Key, *Southern Politics*, chap. 19.

9. Black and Black, "Democratic Gubernatorial Runoff Primaries."

10. Miller, telephone interview with Loch K. Johnson, 1983.

11. Talmadge, *Talmadge*, pp. 343–44.

12. Williams, interview with Loch K. Johnson, Athens, Ga., 1984; Ewing, *Primary Elections in the South*, pp. 93–94.

13. Alexander, "The Double Primary," p. 256.

14. Jacobson, *Politics of Congressional Elections*, p. 111.

15. Ewing, *Primary Elections in the South*, p. 93. Multiple candidate fields, however, do not always mean that the incumbent is a common opponent. Incumbents have been known to recruit a stalking horse whom they anticipate will split the opposition or simply confuse the electorate.

16. Caldwell, *The Caldwell Conspiracy*, p. 51.

17. Ibid., p. 52.

18. Black and Black, "Democratic Gubernatorial Runoff Primaries," p. 20.

19. Jacobson, *Politics of Congressional Elections*.

20. See, for example, Deckard, *Women's Movement*, p. 367.

21. The secondary state offices for which runoffs have been included and the numbers of runoffs are reported in chapter 1.

22. Bullock and Johnson, "Runoff Elections in Georgia," pp. 937–46.

23. Black and Black, "Democratic Gubernatorial Runoff Primaries," p. 10; Key, *Southern Politics*, p. 423.

24. Fleischmann and Stein, "Minority and Female Success," p. 382.

25. Texas provides a potentially important exception, with the number of state senators (31) approximating the number of U.S. House members (23 in 1970; 24 from 1972 to 1980 and 27 from 1982 to 1986) more closely than the number of state house members (150). This means that a Texas state senator has almost as many constituents as a federal representative from Texas and far more than a state representative. Because we were unable to obtain election results for members of the Texas lower house, we could not explore the constituency-contact hypothesis there.

26. Recall that in North Carolina we obtained no data on state legislative primaries.

27. Theodoulou, "Impact of the Open Elections System."

28. On the decline in the number of electorally marginal House districts, see Mayhew, "Congressional Elections" and *The Electoral Connection*; Fiorina, *Congress*. In 1986 and 1988, more than 98 percent of the House incumbents who stood for reelection succeeded.

29. Black and Black, "Democratic Gubernatorial Runoff Primaries."

30. Ibid., pp. 14–17; Merle Black, "Young Faces Long Odds," p. D5.

31. Bullock and Johnson, "Runoff Elections in Georgia," p. 941.

32. Except when reference is made to Ewing's book, the analyses reported on the Ewing Data are based on results we generated after reviewing the materials collected by Ewing and archived at the University of Oklahoma.

33. Ewing, *Primary Elections in the South*, p. 96; Fleischmann and Stein, "Minority and Female Success," p. 382.

34. Because of the small number of statewide contests, caution should be exercised in interpreting these results. Ewing does not report separate figures for state senators and state representatives.

35. Key, *Southern Politics*, pp. 201–4.

36. Alexander, "The Double Primary," p. 264.

37. Park, "The Elusive Majority."

38. Black and Black, "Democratic Gubernatorial Runoff Primaries."

39. Fleischmann and Stein, "Minority and Female Success," p. 382.

40. Fenno, *Home Style*, p. 211.

41. Stanley and Niemi, *Vital Statistics on American Politics*, p. 188; Jewell and Breaux, "Effect of Incumbency."

42. Jacobson and Kernell, *Strategy and Choice*.

43. See, for example, Jacobson, "Incumbents' Advantages."

44. Beginning with the 1986 election, the term for the governor of Arkansas was increased from two to four years. This study, however, ceases with the 1986 round of elections.

45. Over this senator's first decade in office, the number of days in his home state (excluding the August and Christmas recesses) was, in order, 50, 55, 67, 78, 78, 92, 38, 34, 50, and 58.

46. Glenn R. Parker, "Sources of Change."

47. Kuklinski, "Representativeness and Elections," pp. 173–74; Elling, "Ideological Change." While Kuklinski observed a difference in behavior between California senators and state representatives, comparable differences would be unlikely in the states using runoffs as these states typically do not give their senators longer terms than their representatives. Therefore, the finding that the leaders in state senate contests are reelected at slightly higher rates than those in state house contests is not necessarily at variance with Kuklinski's California research.

48. Ewing, *Primary Elections in the South*, p. 93.

49. In 1988 female turnout exceeded male turnout in all the runoff states except North Carolina, although only in Oklahoma were the differences statistically significant (U.S. Bureau of the Census, *Voting and Registration in the Election of November 1988*, 1989, pp. 6–9). In 1986 women voted at higher rates than men in Alabama, Florida, Georgia, Louisiana, and Mississippi with a statistically significant differences

in Florida (U.S. Bureau of the Census, *Voting and Registration in the Election of November 1986*, 1987, pp. 25–27).

50. Smeal, "Eleanor Smeal Report," p. 1.

51. Quoted in Lanier, "The Runoff Primary," p. 22.

52. These data were collected by and described more fully in Bullock and Mac-Manus, "Municipal Electoral Structure."

53. Fleischmann and Stein, "Minority and Female Success," p. 382.

54. See Bullock and Johnson, "Sex and the Second Primary."

55. See Black and Black, "Democratic Gubernatorial Runoff Primaries."

56. Because women who participated in five-person primaries have fared poorly in runoffs, a dummy indicating presence in a five-person field was tried. It proved to be collinear with other predictors and, therefore, was not included in Table 2.19 below.

57. Stanley, "The Runoff," p. 233, n. 7; Lamis, "The Runoff Primary Controversy," p. 783, n. 2 (for Ward).

58. Quoted by Roberts, "Ruing Jackson's Stand on Runoffs."

59. Theodore H. White, "Jackson, Democratic Revolutionary."

60. Ibid.; Lance quoted by Allen, political editor, *Atlanta Constitution*, p. B1.

61. The officials in this paragraph were all quoted in the *New York Times*, May 1, 1984.

62. Julian Bond, "Second Thoughts." Emphasis added.

63. Stanley, "The Runoff," p. 232.

64. See Allen, quoted in *Atlanta Constitution*, p. B1.

65. See Wicker, "Jackson on Wrong Track."

66. Earl Black, *Southern Governors*.

67. Wicker, "Jackson on Wrong Track."

68. Julian Bond, "Second Thoughts"; Stanley, "The Runoff," p. 232.

69. Cavanagh quoted by Fielder, political editor, *Miami Herald*, p. A12; Michaux quoted in Congressional Quarterly, *Weekly Report*, p. 1035.

70. Stanley, "The Runoff," p. 234, n. 7.

71. Julian Bond, "Second Thoughts"; Stanley, "The Runoff," p. 235.

72. Quoted by Fielder, *Miami Herald*, p. A12.

73. Key, *Southern Politics*; Lawson, *Black Ballots* and *In Pursuit of Power*; Kousser, *The Shaping of Southern Politics*; Woodward, *Strange Career of Jim Crow*.

Chapter 3

1. White, "Here Is New York."

2. *New York Times*, April 20, 1972, p. A44.

3. On the experience of black-Hispanic voting, see Bullock and McManus, "Voting Patterns" and "Mexican-American Political Clout"; Butler and Murray, "Minority Vote Dilution Suits."

4. *Butts v. City of New York*, 779 F. 2d 141 (2d Cir. 1985); *Butts v. City of New York*, 614 F. Supp. 1527 (S.D.N.Y. 1985), and the accompanying *Memorandum and Order*, pp. 61–62.

5. Lindsay quoted in *Memorandum and Order* accompanying *Butts v. City of New York*, 614 F. Supp. 1527 (S.D.N.Y. 1985), p. 59.

6. *New York Assembly Journal*, 2:1476–77; *New York Senate Journal*, 2:292–93.

7. *New York Times*, April 15 and 20, 1972, pp. A1, A44. Looking back on the origins of the law, one New York legislator recalls that in his opinion the 40 percent rule would have catapulted Herman Badillo into the mayorship had it been in effect in 1969 in the Proccacino race and had Badillo been the number two candidate: " . . . he would have picked up 75 percent of the vote at that particular time, because he represented a [liberal] political philosophy." Senator Bloom, quoted in Brief of Amicus Curiae, State of New York, *Butts v. City of New York*, U.S. Court of Appeals for the Second Circuit, No. 85-7670 (August 27, 1985), p. 18.

8. Reply Brief for Appellants, *Butts v. City of New York*, U.S. Court of Appeals for the Second Circuit, No. 85-7670 (September 9, 1985), p. 5 n.

9. *Proccacino v. Board of Elections*, 73 Misc. 2d at 470, 341 N.Y.S. 2d at 818 (Sup. Ct. N.Y. Co. 1973).

10. Even when Badillo made it into the runoff in 1973, Sutton declined to support him and Badillo was able to attract only 62 percent of the black vote. Brief of Amicus Curiae, *Butts v. City of New York*, U.S. Court of Appeals for the Second Circuit, No. 85-7670 (September 9, 1985), p. 8, n. 4.

11. Brief of Amicus Curiae, Metropolitan Black Bar Association, ibid. (September 4, 1985), p. 3.

12. Brief of Amicus Curiae, NAACP Legal Defense Educational Fund, ibid. (September 4, 1985), p. 16.

13. Ibid. (June 3–10, 1985), p. 90.

14. Ibid., p. 122.

15. Reply Brief for Appellants, ibid. (September 9, 1985), p. 15 n.

16. Ibid., p. 121.

17. Ibid., p. 52.

18. Dr. Ester Fuchs, a political scientist at Barnard College and expert witness for the defendants, ibid., p. 713.

19. Ibid., pp. 222–23.

20. *Memorandum and Order*, ibid., September 9, 1985, pp. 33, 43.

21. *Butts v. City of New York*, No. 84 7373-CLB, slip opinion at 51 (S.D.N.Y. August 13, 1985).

22. Amicus Curiae Brief, State of New York, *Butts v. City of New York*, U.S. Court of Appeals for the Second Circuit, No. 85-7670 (August 27, 1985), pp. 6–9, 20 (quotation), 74–75.

23. Ibid., pp. 32, 31, 42.

24. Brief for Appellants, City of New York, *Butts v. City of New York*, U.S. Court of Appeals for the Second Circuit, No. 85–7670 (August 27, 1985), pp. 3–4.

25. Ibid., p. 31.

26. Ibid., p. 47.

27. *Butts v. City of New York*, 779 F. 2d 141 (2d Cir. 1985).

28. Dissenting Opinion, ibid., pp. 2, 5.

29. Ibid., p. 7, notes, p. iii.

30. *Whitfield v. Democratic Party of the State of Arkansas*, 686 F. Supp. 1365 (E.D. Ark. 1988). The following account is based on the research of Alexander, "The Double Primary," as cited in ibid.

31. See Alexander, ibid., p. 232.

32. Stanley, "Runoff Primaries," p. 270, table 14.3.

33. *Whitfield*, 686 F. Supp. 1365 (E.D. Ark. 1988) (quotations, pp. 1371, 1370, 1373).

34. Ibid., p. 1371.

35. Ibid., pp. 1373, 1376.

36. Ibid., p. 1378.

37. Ibid., p. 1376.

38. Ibid., p. 1379.

39. *Whitfield v. Democratic Party of the State of Arkansas*, No. 88–1953 (8th Cir., December 7, 1989).

40. It is well established that in determining a Section 2 violation, the outcome is not premised on a simple counting of the elements for and against the claim of dilution. The Supreme Court in *Thornburg v. Gingles* (478 U.S. 30 [1986]) has identified some elements as particularly important. A finding of racially polarized voting, for example, is essential to any determination of a violation of Section 2. Also important is the incidence of minority candidates who have been elected in the jurisdiction.

41. Quoted in Wells, "Lawyer Partially Wins," p. 28.

42. Quoted in Wells, "Runoff Ruling Termed 'Historic,' " p. 18.

43. *Jeffers v. Clinton*, No. H.C.-89-004 (E.D. Ark., May 16, 1990).

44. Ibid., p. 25.

Chapter 4

1. Cited in "Run-Off Primaries Discriminatory," *Cleveland Plain Dealer*, August 18, 1985, p. B4.

2. Adolph Reed asserts that it was Michaux who urged Jackson to make an issue of runoff elections. Reed, *The Jesse Jackson Phenomenon*, p. 76. Some chroniclers of the 1984 Jackson presidential campaign, including Reed, believe the emphasis on the runoff to have been misplaced. See also McCormick, "Anatomy of a Tactical Miscalculation."

3. An alternative perspective on the Hall defeat is offered by Louis Maisel, who notes that Hall came within 2,000 votes of achieving a plurality. Maisel concludes that the plurality standard was positive for Hall even though she failed to finish first because "she could not have achieved a majority." Maisel, *From Obscurity to Oblivion*, pp. 142–43. Of course, no one can know what would have happened had a runoff rule been in place. It is highly probable, however, that had Hall been offered an opportunity to go one-on-one with primary leader Peter Visclosky in a runoff, she would have leaped at the chance.

4. McTeer, Testimony, *Hearings, Voting Rights Act*, pp. 29, 31.

5. Thurmond, interview with Loch K. Johnson, Athens, Ga., March 22, 1990.

6. Simpson, "The Primary Runoff," p. 369.

7. When Andrew Young first received the Democratic nomination to Congress from Atlanta in 1970, he won a runoff in a majority white district. He subsequently lost the general election. In 1972 Young was nominated and elected from a 44 percent black district.

8. According to the 1980 Census, Allen Wheat, a Democrat from Kansas City, represented a district that was 23 percent black; Ron Dellums (D-Calif.) came from a district that was 60 percent black. For an enumeration of minority black districts that have sent blacks to Congress, see Swain, "The Politics of Black Representation."

9. Quoted in Willis, "Zell Miller's Triple Image," C2.

10. Stanley, "The Runoff"; McDonald, "The Majority Vote Requirement," pp. 435–36.

11. Canon, "Factionalism in the South."

12. Kousser, Testimony, *County Council of Sumter County*.

13. Barnes, "End the Georgia Runoff?" (quotation); Woolner, "Hosea Williams Changes Mind," p. A30.

14. McDonald, "The Majority Vote Requirement," p. 435, and Statement, *Hearings, Voting Rights Act*, p. 84.

15. *Voting Rights Act*, pp. 1746–82.

16. McTeer, Testimony, *Hearings, Voting Rights Act*, p. 43; Kousser, "Historical Origins"; McDonald, "The Majority Vote Requirement," p. 429.

17. McCrary, Deposition, *Hall v. Holder*, p. 43; Simpson, "The Primary Runoff," p. 375.

18. Alexander, "The Double Primary," p. 265.

19. Stanley, "Runoff Primaries," pp. 268–69.

20. For example, despite extended discussion of the poll tax, literacy test, and white primary, no coverage is given to the runoff in Kousser, *The Shaping of Southern Politics.*

21. Key, *Southern Politics*, p. 417; Keech and Swain, "The Southern Runoff Primary Controversy"; Citizens Union of New York City, "Legislative Memorandum," p. 1; *New York Times* editorial quoted in Fuchs, "Report on the New York Runoff Primary" (second quotation).

22. Foster, Testimony, *Hearings, Voting Rights Act*, p. 5.

23. McCrary, Testimony, *Dent v. Culpepper.*

24. McDonald, Statement, *Hearings, Voting Rights Act*, pp. 103, 82.

25. Suitts, Statement, *Hearings, Voting Rights Act*, p. 70.

26. Foster, Testimony, *Hearings, Voting Rights Act*, pp. 5–6; Suitts, Statement, *Hearings, Voting Rights Act*, pp. 71–72.

27. See, for example, McTeer, Testimony, *Hearings, Voting Rights Act*, pp. 28–28.

28. Bullock and MacManus, "Structural Features of Municipal Elections."

29. Fuchs, "Report on the New York Runoff," pp. 9–10.

30. For a fuller discussion see Bullock and Smith, "Black Success in Local Runoff Elections," from which the data in the remainder of this section are drawn.

31. *Voting Rights Act*; Derfner, "The 'Second Primary.' "

32. A voting rights attorney at the Joint Center for Political Studies in Washington, D.C., argues that "Atlanta politics are atypical of what's happening throughout the South. Everywhere else, the runoff primary works to keep blacks out of office at almost every level." Frank Parker (*Montgomery* [Ala.] *Journal and Advertiser*).

Chapter 5

1. "In Step with the Times," Raleigh *News and Observer*, July 7, 1989.

2. Christensen, "Primary Runoff Law Modified." The potential for a coalition of blacks and Republicans in North Carolina has a less lengthy history than in some other southern states. In a number of other states, a GOP-black coalition was active during the post-1980 redistricting battles but seems not to have emerged in North Carolina. Bullock, "Redistricting and Changes." The two ideologically distant groups did, however, join forces in a 1987 challenge to the state's multimember superior court arrangement.

3. In 1991 a member of the Black Caucus was elected speaker of the North Carolina House—the most powerful position achieved by a black legislator in the South.

4. Christensen, "Change in the Primary System Debated."

5. Flesher, "Primary Vote Law Passed." Michaux became the cause célèbre of the antirunoff effort when his 1982 plurality in a congressional primary failed to lead to a nomination.

6. Quoted in Christensen, "Black Democrats Revive Limits."

7. "Panel OKs Bill to Allow Fewer 2nd Primaries," *Greensboro News and Record*, June 24, 1989.

8. Christensen, "Change in the Primary System Debated."

9. Lineberry, "Senate OKs Bill to Cut Run-Offs."

10. Lineberry, "Bill to End Runoffs Gains in N.C. Senate," p. A2.

11. Quoted in Christensen, "Change in the Primary System Debated."

12. Quoted in "Panel Amends Bill to Change System for Runoff Elections," *Winston-Salem Journal*, June 21, 1989.

13. Lineberry, "House Subcommittee Guts Primary Bill," p. A2.

14. Quoted in Christensen, "Change in the Primary System Debated," and Flesher, "Primary Vote Law Passed," pp. B1–B2.

15. Quoted in "Bill to Let Candidates Win Primaries without Majority Is Passed by House," *Winston-Salem Journal*, July 1, 1989. Also subscribing to this view are Jones and Johnston, "The Forty Percent Rule."

16. Christensen, "Primary Runoff Law Modified," p. A4.

17. Canon, "Factionalism In the South"; Stanley, "The Runoff: The Case for Retention."

18. Dunne quoted in Smothers, "U.S. Files Suit against Georgia," p. A13; Jones and Johnston, "The Forty Percent Rule," pp. 4, 9.

19. Quoted in Christensen, "Change in the Primary System Debated."

20. The data discussed in this section relies on Jones and Johnston, "The Forty Percent Rule."

21. Ibid., p. 22.

Chapter 6

1. Janice Thurmond, quoted in Lo Monte, "Young Charts Plans for Bucking Odds," p. 1.

2. Baxter, "The Legacy of Young's Campaign," p. G2. The black candidate lost the runoff with 40 percent of the vote after trailing in the initial primary. Districtwide, turnout in the runoff fell by 5 percent from the first primary. Because the black candidate failed to poll a plurality in any county in the initial primary or a majority in any county in the second primary, higher turnout in three of the five counties in the runoff probably did not determine the outcome.

3. Quoted in Barnes, "Liberal Trend Pleases GOP in South." Darden refers to the runoff following a first primary that eliminated the three most conservative candidates.

4. Foster, Testimony, *Hearings, Voting Rights Act*, p. 7.

5. Lanier, "The Runoff Primary," p. 21.

6. Ibid., p. 22.

7. Simana, Public Address.

8. Black and Black, *Politics and Society in the South*.

9. Key, *Southern Politics*, p. 417; Keech and Swain, "The Southern Runoff Primary Controversy," p. 13.

10. Keech and Swain, "The Southern Runoff Primary Controversy," p. 15; Haeberle, "Rundown on the Runoff."

11 Black and Black, "Democratic Gubernatorial Runoff Primaries."

12. Smith, *The Electorate in an Alabama Community*, cited in Alexander, "The Double Primary," p. 262.

13. Alexander, "The Double Primary," p. 262.

14. Wright, "Voter Turnout."

15. Lanier, "The Runoff Primary," pp. 18–23, reports lower participation in runoffs than primaries in eighteen of twenty-three pairs of contests he studied.

16. Wright, "Voter Turnout," also reports high dropoffs for Texas runoffs.

17. Lanier, "The Runoff Primary."

18. On Louisiana's primary system, see Theodoulou, "Impact of the Open Elections System."

19. In an effort to make data for Louisiana as similar as possible to those for other states, only second contests in which both candidates were of the same party are included in this and other analyses.

20. Washington won a plurality in the Democratic primary and the general election; Massell lost the runoff. Washington quoted in "Chicago's Morning After."

21. Wright, "Voter Turnout."

22. Bullock, "Turnout in Municipal Elections."

23. Throughout this chapter comparisons of turnout are between runoffs and primaries and not across offices. Thus, the relative participation levels across pairs of elections are more similar for offices farther down the ballot. The actual share of the electorate going to the polls may be greater for more visible contests at the top of the ballot. We do not have the data needed to explore relative turnout across offices.

24. The 1990 gubernatorial runoff, which featured the two more liberal candidates from the first primary, saw a drop of 96,000 voters. The decline may bespeak alienation among the supporters of three more conservative aspirants eliminated by the initial balloting. The biracial nature of the runoff in which former Atlanta mayor Andrew Young polled 38 percent of the vote against Lieutenant Governor Zell Miller showed no antiblack mobilization in the electorate.

Chapter 7

1. Keech and Swain, "The Southern Runoff Primary Controversy," p. 15.

2. Haeberle, "Rundown on the Runoff."

3. Although it is possible that Republicans might have felt betrayed by the fickle Graddick, this seems not to have been a concern. Moreover, Fob James, Alabama's governor from 1979 to 1983, had beaten Baxley in a runoff two years after he (James) had served on the GOP state executive committee.

4. Young, Deposition, *Brooks v. Harris*.

5. Black and Black, "Democratic Gubernatorial Runoff Primaries," pp. 5–6.

6. Ibid.

7. Bullock and Smith, "Black Success in Local Runoff Elections," p. 1217.

8. Haeberle, "Rundown on the Runoff," p. 17.

9. Quoted in Cummings and May, "Twenty-seven File Suit," p. A1.

10. Quoted in Cummings, "Challenge of Runoff Systems," p. A1.

11. The state was ill prepared to implement its new legislation. Only after it became clear that no one had a majority in the 1990 gubernatorial election was the procedure for carrying out a runoff established.

12. Much of the material on Kentucky was kindly provided by Al Cross, political writer for the *Louisville Courier-Journal*. We greatly appreciate his assistance.

13. Cross, "Senate Approves Bill," p. A1.

14. Cross, "Runoffs Considered," p. A14.

15. Subsequently, Martha Wilkinson did enter the 1991 gubernatorial contest but withdrew when it became obvious that she would not be nominated.

16. In 1980 Kentucky was only 7 percent black so that, unlike in some states that have a majority-vote provision, it would be virtually impossible for a black running statewide to be a plurality winner by relying exclusively on black support. (In Georgia, for example, the black population is 27 percent.)

17. Quoted in Cross, "Senate Approves Bill."

Bibliography

Alexander, Henry M. 1944. "The Double Primary." *Arkansas Historical Quarterly* 3: 217–68.

Allen, Frederick. 1984. Quoted in *Atlanta Constitution*, May 1.

Aylsworth, Leon E. 1909. "Primary Elections, Majority Nominations, and the Second Voice Ballot." *American Political Science Review* 2: 563–65.

Barnes, James A. 1990a. "End the Georgia Runoff? Not for Young." *National Journal* 22: 1229.

———. 1990b. "Liberal Trend Pleases GOP in South." *National Journal* 22: 1673.

Baxter, Tom. 1988. "Second Place a Position to Envy in Fla. Democratic Senate Race." *Atlanta Constitution*, September 3.

———. 1990. "The Legacy of Young's Campaign." *Atlanta Constitution*, August 12.

Black, Duncan. 1958. *The Theory of Committees and Elections*. London: Cambridge University Press.

Black, Earl. 1976. *Southern Governors and Civil Rights*. Cambridge: Harvard University Press.

———. 1983. "A Theory of Southern Factionalism." *Journal of Politics* 45: 594–614.

Black, Earl, and Merle Black. 1987. *Politics and Society in the South*. Cambridge: Harvard University Press.

Black, Merle. 1990. "Young Faces Long Odds in Democratic Runoff with Miller." *Atlanta Journal-Constitution*, July 22.

Black, Merle, and Earl Black. 1976. "Republican Party Development in the South: The Rise of the Contested Primary." *Social Science Quarterly* 57: 566–78.

———. 1987. "Democratic Gubernatorial Runoff Primaries in the Modern South." Paper presented at the annual meeting of the American Political Science Association, Chicago, Ill., September 3–6.

Bond, John R. 1983. "The Influence of Constituency Diversity on Electoral Competition in Voting for Congress, 1974–1978." *Legislative Studies Quarterly* 8: 201–17.

Bond, Julian. 1984. "Second Thoughts on the Runoffs." *Atlanta Constitution*, May 1.

Bullock, Charles S., III. 1977. "Explaining Congressional Elections: Differences in Perceptions of Opposing Candidates." *Legislative Studies Quarterly* 2: 295–308.

———. 1987. "Redistricting and Changes in the Partisan and Racial Composition of Southern Legislatures." *State and Local Government Review* 19: 62–67.

———. 1988. "Creeping Realignment in the South." In *The South's New Politics*, edited by Robert H. Swansbrough and David M. Brodsky, pp. 220–37. Columbia: University of South Carolina Press.

———. 1990. "Turnout in Municipal Elections." *Policy Studies Review* 9: 539–49.

Bullock, Charles S., III, and Loch K. Johnson. 1985. "Runoff Elections in Georgia." *Journal of Politics* 47: 936–46.

———. 1985. "Sex and the Second Primary," *Social Science Quarterly* 66: 933–44.

———. 1987. "The Incidence of Runoff Primaries." In *Blacks in Southern Politics*, edited by Laurence W. Moreland, Robert P. Steed, and Tod A. Baker, pp. 277–92. New York: Praeger.

Bullock, Charles S., III, and Susan A. MacManus. 1986. "Mexican- American Political Clout in Small Urban Jurisdictions: Conditions for Maximizing Influence." In *The Equalitarian City*, edited by Janet K. Boles, pp. 17–26. New York: Praeger.

———. 1987. "Structural Features of Municipal Elections and Black Descriptive Representation." Paper presented at the annual meeting of the Southern Political Science Association, Charlotte, N.C., November 5–7.

———. 1990. "Voting Patterns in a Tri-Ethnic Community: Conflict or Cohesion? The Case of Austin, Texas, 1975–1985." *National Civic Review* 79: 5–22.

———. 1991. "Municipal Electoral Structure and the Election of Councilwomen." *Journal of Politics* 53: 76–89.

Bullock, Charles S., III, and A. Brock Smith. 1990. "Black Success in Local Runoff Elections." *Journal of Politics* 52: 1205–22.

Butler, Katherine I., and Richard Murray. 1990. "Minority Vote Dilution Suits and the Problem of Two Minority Groups: Can a 'Rainbow Coalition' Claim the Protection of the Voting Rights Act?" *Pacific Law Review* 21: 619–89.

Butts v. City of New York. 1985. U.S. Court of Appeals for the Second Circuit, no. 85-7670.

Caldwell, Sam. 1987. *The Caldwell Conspiracy*. Lakemont, Ga.: Cobbell House.

Canon, Bradley C. 1978. "Factionalism in the South: A Test and a Revisitation of V. O. Key." *American Journal of Political Science* 22: 833–48.

"Chicago's Morning After." 1983. *The New Republic*, May 2, p. 8.

Christensen, Rob. 1989a. "Change in the Primary System Debated." Raleigh *News and Observer*, May 13.

———. 1989b. "Black Democrats Revive Limits on Runoff Primaries." Raleigh *News and Observer*, June 28.

———. 1989c. "Primary Runoff Law Modified." Raleigh *News and Observer*, July 1.

Citizens Union of New York City. 1984. "Legislative Memorandum: Repeal of New York City Mayoral Runoff and Survey of Mayoral Candidacies in Major American Cities." May 1.

Claybrook, Clint. 1992. Telephone interview, recalling an interview by him and his colleague Jim Lynn in 1988.

Congressional Quarterly. 1956–91. *Weekly Reports*.

——— 1985. *Guide to U.S. Elections*. 2d ed. Washington, D.C.: Congressional Quarterly.

Cross, Al. 1990a. "Runoffs Considered for 1991 Statewide Races." *Louisville Courier-Journal*, January 20.

———. 1990b. "Senate Approves Bill Setting Primary Runoff for Governor, Lieutenant." *Louisville Courier-Journal*, February 3.

Cummings, Jeanne. 1990. "Challenge of Runoff Systems Could Benefit Republicans." *Atlanta Journal*, May 10.

Cummings, Jeanne, and A. L. May. 1990. "Twenty-seven File Suit Alleging Runoff Law Dilutes Black Voting Strength." *Atlanta Constitution*, May 9.

Deckard, Barbara Sinclair. 1983. *The Women's Movement*. 3d ed. New York: Harper and Row.

Derfner, Armand. N.d. "The 'Second Primary' or 'Majority Vote Requirement.' " Unpublished paper discussed in Laughlin McDonald, "The Majority Vote Requirement: Its Use and Abuse in the South," *Urban Lawyer* 17: 432–33.

Duncan, Phil. 1984. "Jackson's Anti-Runoff Push Divides Southern Democrats." *Congressional Quarterly Weekly Report* 42: 1033–35.

Durbin, Thomas M. 1984. "Runoff Elections and the Voting Rights Act of 1965 as Amended." Washington, D.C.: Congressional Research Service.

Elling, Richard C. 1982. "Ideological Change in the U.S. Senate: Time and Electoral Responsiveness." *Legislative Studies Quarterly* 7: 75–92.

Ewing, Cortez A. M. 1980. *Primary Elections in the South: A Study in Uniparty Politics*. Norman: University of Oklahoma Press, 1953. Reprint. Westport, Conn.: Greenwood.

Fenno, Richard F. 1978. *Home Style*. Boston: Little, Brown.

Fielder, Tom. 1984. *Miami Herald*, April 15.

Fiorina, Morris. 1977. *Congress: Keystone of the Washington Establishment*. New Haven: Yale University Press.

Fishburn, Peter C., and Steven J. Brams. 1981. "Approval Voting, Condorcet's Principle, and Runoff Elections." *Public Choice* 36: 89–114.

Fleischmann, Arnold, and Lana Stein. 1987. "Minority and Female Success in Municipal Runoff Elections." *Social Science Quarterly* 68: 378–85.

Flesher, John. 1989. "Primary Vote Law Passed." *Greensboro News and Record*, July 1.

Foster, Lorn. 1985. Testimony. *Hearings, Voting Rights Act: Runoff Primaries and Registration Barriers*. Subcommittee on Civil and Constitutional Rights, Committee on the Judiciary, U.S. House of Representatives. 98th Cong., 2d sess. Washington, D.C.: U.S. Government Printing Office.

———. 1988. "Runoff Primaries." In *Capital Court House and City Hall*, 7th ed., edited by David L. Martin. New York: Longman.

Fuchs, Ester. 1985. In "Report on the New York Runoff Primary," prepared by defendants in *Butts v. City of New York* (779 F. 2d 141; 2d Cir. 1985), pp. 9–14.

Haeberle, Steven H. 1987. "Rundown on the Runoff: Party Runaway Run Amok." Paper presented at the annual meeting of the Southern Political Science Association, Charlotte, N.C., November 5–7.

Havard, William C. 1972. *The Changing Politics of the South*. Baton Rouge: Louisiana State University Press.

Jackson, Jesse. 1984a. "Moving to the Common Ground." *Washington Post* (National ed.), April 9.

———. 1984b. "Runoffs and Voting Rights." *Washington Post*, April 16.

———. 1984c. "Rainbow Coalition Is a Success." *Atlanta Journal-Constitution*, April 22.

Jacobson, Gary C. 1981. "Incumbents' Advantages in the 1978 Congressional Elections." *Legislative Studies Quarterly* 6: 183–200.

———. 1987. *The Politics of Congressional Elections*. 2d ed. Boston: Little, Brown.

Jacobson, Gary C., and Samuel Kernell. 1983. *Strategy and Choice in Congressional Elections*. New Haven: Yale University Press.

Jewell, Malcolm, and David Breaux. 1988. "The Effect of Incumbency on State Legislative Elections." *Legislative Studies Quarterly* 13: 495–514.

Joint Center for Political Studies. 1984. *Background Paper: Run-Off Primaries*. Washington, D.C.: Joint Center for Political Studies.

Jones, Lloyd P., and W. Lee Johnston. 1990. "The Forty Percent Rule and North Carolina Runoff Elections: An Initial Analysis." Paper presented at the annual meeting of the Southern Political Science Association, Atlanta, Ga., November 8–10.

Keech, William R., and Carol M. Swain. 1986. "The Southern Runoff Primary Controversy." Paper presented at the annual meeting of the Southern Political Science Association, Atlanta, Ga., November 6–8.

Key, V. O., Jr. 1949. *Southern Politics in State and Nation*. New York: Knopf.

Kousser, J. Morgan. 1974. *The Shaping of Southern Politics*. New Haven: Yale University Press.

———. 1984a. Testimony. *County Council of Sumter County, S.C. v. U.S.* (Ca. No. 82–0912). February 18, pp. 912–13.

———. 1984b. "The Historical Origins of the Run-Off Primary." *Focus* 12: 7–9.

Kuklinski, James H. 1978. "Representativeness and Elections: A Policy Analysis." *American Political Science Review* 72: 165–77.

Ladd, Everett Carll, Jr. 1970. *American Political Parties: Social Change and Political Response*. New York: Norton.

Lamis, Alexander P. 1984. "The Runoff Primary Controversy: Implications for Southern Politics." *PS* 17: 782–87.

Lanier, Mark. 1983. "The Runoff Primary: A Path to Victory." *N.C. Insight*. June: 18–23.

Lawson, Steven F. 1976. *Black Ballots*. New York: Columbia University Press.

———. 1985. *In Pursuit of Power*. New York: Columbia University Press.

Liebling, A. J. 1960, 1970. *The Earl of Louisiana*. Baton Rouge: Louisiana State University Press.

Lineberry, Danny. 1989a. "Bill to End Runoffs Gains in N.C. Senate." *Durham Morning Herald*, April 20.

———. 1989b. "Senate OKs Bill to Cut Run-Offs." *Durham Morning Herald*, April 28.

———. 1989c. "House Subcommittee Guts Primary Bill." *Durham Morning Herald*, June 21.

Lo Monte, Frank. 1990. "Young Charts Plans for Bucking Odds." *Athens Banner-Herald*, July 19.

Lush, Charles K. 1908. "Primary Elections and Majority Nominations." *American Political Science Review*. 2: 43–47.

McCormick, Joseph P., II. 1986. "Anatomy of a Tactical Miscalculation: Jesse Jackson's Challenge to the Second Primary System." Paper presented at the Conference on the Social and Political Implications of the Jesse Jackson Presidential Campaign, Washington, D.C., March 27–28.

McCrary, Peyton. 1987. Testimony. *Dent v. Culpepper*, pp. 88–89.

———. 1987. Deposition. *Hall v. Holder*.

MacDonald, Austin F. 1940. "American Government and Politics." *American Political Science Review* 34: 499–506.

McDonald, Laughlin. 1983. "The 1982 Extension of Section 5 of the Voting Rights Act of 1965: A Continued Need for PreClearance." *Tennessee Law Review* 51: 1–82.

———. 1985a. "The Majority Vote Requirement: Its Use and Abuse in the South." *Urban Lawyer* 17: 429–39.

———. 1985b. Statement. *Hearings, Voting Rights Act: Runoff Primaries and Registration Barriers*. Subcommittee on Civil and Constitutional Rights, Committee on the Judiciary, U.S. House of Representatives. 98th Cong., 2d sess. Washington, D.C.: U.S. Government Printing Office.

McTeer, Victor. 1985. Testimony. *Hearings, Voting Rights Act: Runoff Primaries and Registration Barriers*. Subcommittee on Civil and Constitutional Rights, Committee on the Judiciary, U.S. House of Representatives. 98th Cong., 2d sess. Washington, D.C.: U.S. Government Printing Office.

Maisel, Louis Sandy. 1986. *From Obscurity to Oblivion*. Rev. ed. Knoxville: University of Tennessee Press.

Mayhew, David R. 1974a. "Congressional Elections: The Case of the Vanishing Marginals." *Polity* 6: 295–317.

———. 1974b. *The Electoral Connection*. New Haven: Yale University Press.

Merrill, Samuel, III. 1984. "A Comparison of Efficiency of Multicandidate Electoral Systems." *American Journal of Political Science* 28: 23–48.

———. 1988. *Making Multicandidate Elections More Democratic*. Princeton, N.J.: Princeton University Press.

Mollison, Andrew. 1984. "Jackson Calls for a New Coalition." *Atlanta Journal-Constitution*, November 4.

Murphy, Lionel V. 1933. "Two Trials of Oklahoma's Runoff Primary." *Southwestern Social Science Quarterly* 14: 156–74.

Newsbank Electronic Information System. 1981–91. "Runoff Elections." Microfiche. Athens: University of Georgia Library.

New York Assembly Journal. 1972. 195th sess., vol. 2.

New York Senate Journal. 1972. 195th sess., vol. 2.

Overacker, Louise. 1940. "Direct Primary Legislation, 1936–1939." *American Political Science Review* (June): 503–6.

Park, Joe. 1940. "The Elusive Majority." *National Municipal Review*. October: 675–78.

Parker, Frank. 1985. Interview. *Montgomery* (Ala.) *Journal and Advertiser*, August 15.

Parker, Glenn R. 1980. "Sources of Change in Congressional District Attentiveness." *American Journal of Political Science* 24: 115–24.

————. 1989. "Members of Congress and Their Constituents: The Home-Style Connection." In *Congress Reconsidered*, 4th ed., edited by Lawrence C. Dodd and Bruce I. Oppenheimer, pp. 171–93. Washington, D.C.: Congressional Quarterly.

Reed, Adolph L., Jr. 1986. *The Jesse Jackson Phenomenon*. New Haven: Yale University Press.

Riker, William H. 1982. *Liberalism against Populism*. San Francisco: Freeman.

Roberts, Steven. 1984. "Ruing Jackson's Stand on Runoffs." *New York Times*, April 16.

Schantz, Harvey L. 1980. "Contested and Uncontested Primaries for the U.S. House." *Legislative Studies Quarterly* 5: 545–62.

Sherman, Mark. 1988. "Samples, 24, Tops Byron in District 9 Runoff Upset." *Atlanta Constitution*, October 25.

Simana, Jibari. 1989. Public Address. University of Georgia, Athens, January 19.

Simpson, William. 1984. "The Primary Runoff: Racism's Reprieve?" *North Carolina Law Review* 65: 359–99.

Smeal, Eleanor. 1984. "Eleanor Smeal Report." *Eleanor Smeal Newsletter*, June 28, p. 1.

Smith, Charles W. 1942. *The Electorate in an Alabama Community*. Tuscaloosa: Bureau of Public Administration.

Smothers, Ronald. 1990. "U.S. Files Suit against Georgia." *New York Times*, August 10.

Stanley, Harold W. 1985. "The Runoff: The Case for Retention." *PS* 18: 231–36.

————. 1987. "Runoff Primaries and Black Political Influence." In *Blacks in Southern Politics*, edited by Laurence W. Moreland, Robert P. Steed, and Tod A. Baker, pp. 259–76. New York: Praeger.

Stanley, Harold W., and Richard G. Niemi. 1990. *Vital Statistics on American Politics*. 2d ed. Washington, D.C.: Congressional Quarterly.

Stanley, Harold W., William T. Bianco, and Richard G. Niemi. 1986. "Partisanship and Group Support over Time: A Multivariate Analysis." *American Political Science Review* 80: 969–76.

Steed, Robert P., Tod A. Baker, and Laurence W. Moreland, eds. 1980. *Party Politics in the South*. New York: Praeger.

Suitts, Steven. 1985. Statement. *Hearings, Voting Rights Act: Runoff Primaries and Registration Barriers*. Subcommittee on Civil and Constitutional Rights, Committee on the Judiciary, U.S. House of Representatives. 98th Cong., 2d sess. Washington, D.C.: U.S. Government Printing Office.

Swain, Carol M. 1989. "The Politics of Black Representation in U.S. Congressional Districts." Paper presented at the annual meeting of the Southern Political Science Association, Memphis, Tenn., November 2–4.

Talmadge, Herman E. 1987. *Talmadge: A Political Legacy, a Politician's Life*. Atlanta: Peachtree Press.

Theodoulou, Stella Z. 1985. "The Impact of the Open Elections System and Runoff Primary: A Case Study of Louisiana Electoral Politics, 1975–1984." *Urban Lawyer* 17: 457–71.

Thielemann, Gregory S. N.d. "The Rise and Stall of Southern Republicans in Congress." Unpublished paper.

Thomas, Martin. 1985. "Election Proximity and Senatorial Roll Call Voting." *American Journal of Political Science* 29: 96–111.

Thurmond, Janice. 1990. Quoted in Frank LoMonte, "Young Charts Plans for Bucking Odds," *Athens Banner-Herald*, July 19.

U.S. Bureau of the Census. 1987. *Voting and Registration in the Election of November 1986*. Current Population Reports, ser. P-20, no. 414. Washington, D.C.: U.S. Government Printing Office.

U.S. Bureau of the Census. 1989. *Voting and Registration in the Election of November 1988*. (Advance report), Current Population Reports, ser. P-20, no. 435. Washington, D.C.: U.S. Government Printing Office.

U.S. House of Representatives. 1982. *Extension of the Voting Rights Act*. Washington, D.C.: U.S. Government Printing Office.

Wallace, E. Colette. 1985. "Runoff Primaries: Is There a Discriminatory Result?" *Journal of Law and Politics*. Fall: 369–403.

Weeks, O. Douglas. 1932. "The Texas Direct Primary System." *Southwestern Social Science Quarterly* 13: 95–120.

———. 1948. "The White Primary: 1944–1948." *American Political Science Review* 42: 500–10.

Wells, George. 1989a. "Lawyer Partially Wins." *Arkansas Gazette*, December 8.

———. 1989b. "Runoff Ruling Termed 'Historic.' " *Arkansas Gazette*, December 9.

White, E. B. 1949 "Here Is New York." *Holiday* 5: 34–41.

White, Theodore H. 1984. "Jackson, Democratic Revolutionary." *New York Times*, April 5.

Wicker, Tom. 1984. "Jackson on Wrong Track with Runoff Issue." *New York Times*. May 1.

Willis, Ken. 1980. "Zell Miller's Triple Image Could Confuse the Voters." *Atlanta Constitution*, July 30.

Wright, Stephen G. 1987. "The Number of Candidates and the Merits of Runoff and Plurality Systems." Paper presented at the annual meeting of the Southern Political Science Association, Charlotte, N.C., November 5–7.

———. 1989. "Voter Turnout in Runoff Elections." *Journal of Politics* 51: 385–96.

Wright, Stephen G., and William H. Riker. 1989. "Plurality and Runoff Elections and Numbers of Candidates." *Public Choice* 60: 155–76.

Woodward, C. Vann. 1957. *The Strange Career of Jim Crow*. New York: Oxford University Press.

Woolner, Ann. 1984. "Hosea Williams Changes Mind on Opposing a Primary Runoff." *Atlanta Constitution*, July 12.

Young, Andrew J., Jr. 1990. Deposition. *Brooks v. Harris* (Civil Action No. 1: 90-CV-1001-RCF), June 26.

Index

www.ingramcontent.com/pod-product-compliance
Lightning Source LLC
Chambersburg PA
CBHW020350270326
41926CB00007B/373